ACKNOWLEDGMENTS

Every attempt has been made to credit the sources of copyrighted material used in this book. If any such acknowledgment has been inadvertently omitted or miscredited, receipt of such information would be appreciated.

"Sweet Kitty," by Gary Shiebler, is used by permission of the author.

"Her Own Song," by Mary Alice Baumgardner, is used by permission of the author.

"Love for Sale," "Another Day Was Born," "Woe Be to Me," "A Message From the Birds," "Old Man Moreland" and "Celebrate the Day," by Nancy B. Gibbs, are used by permission of the author.

"Mama Cat," by Lynn Seely, is used by permission of the author.

"Working Overtime," "The Education of Pinkie," "Millie" and "It Was a Bad Idea All Along or How I Came to Bathe a Mouse," by Thirza Peevey, are used by permission of the author.

"Back to School," by Mary M. Alward, is used by permission of the author.

"Spring Threshold" is from *A Feathered Family*, by Linda Johns. Copyright © 1999 by Linda Johns. Published by Sierra Club Books, in conjunction with Crown Publishers, New York, New York.

"Small Miracles," "Alberta," "Eureka!" and "The Night Buster Was a Dolphin," by Lonnie Hull DuPont, are used by permission of the author.

"Yes, I Have Known Love," "A Jingle of Praise" and "Hey! White Kitty!" by Diane M. Ciarloni, are used by permission of the author.

"Just an Ordinary Cat," by Lorrie Kreigsch, is used by permission of the author.

"Disney: Love of My Life," by Toni Eames, is used by permission of the author.

"A Hero for All Seasons," by Carol Fleischman, is used by permission of the author.

"Fine Feathered Friends," by Gina Romsdahl, is used by permission of the author.

"Sweet As Sugar," by Jan Rogers, is used by permission of the author.

"A Very Special Teacher," by Jean M. Fogle, is from *Dog Fancy* magazine, July 2000.

"The Sound of Trouble's Sorrow," by Carolyn Cahill, is used by permission of the author.

"Shadow & Soul" and "The Sweetest of Bears," by T. J. Banks, are used by permission of the author.

"Two Gray Doves," by Anne Watkins, is used by permission of the author.

"Misty and His Guardian Angel" is from *Touched By All Creatures*, by Gay L. Balliet. Copyright © 1999 by Gay L. Balliet. Published by New Horizon Press.

"A Promise on Paws," by Leigh Singh, is used by permission of the author.

"Snowy," by Alice C. Bateman, is used by permission of the author.

(continued on page 208)

Designed by SMS Typography
Illustrations by Michelle Lester
Jacket designed by Dennis Arnold
Printed in the United States of America

Listening to the Animals

SOUL
MENDERS

EDITED BY PHYLLIS HOBE

A GUIDEPOSTS BOOK

Contents

I'M RIGHT HERE

DON'T BE AFRAID

LET ME HELP YOU

CHEER UP!

Introduction

In life's more difficult moments, we often don't know how to help each other. We want to make the pain go away. We search for answers to our questions. We want to fix things that are broken. And we want to do all these things quickly so that we can see each other smile again. Quite often we're disappointed because, in spite of our best efforts, the hurt is still there. No smiles, no new beginnings. The soul is still wounded.

But let an animal come upon the scene and something happens. It happens quietly. The animal simply gets close and settles down, inviting a hand to reach out and feel its warmth and love. In time, tears may fall—good tears, the kind that let the hurt come out. Eventually, there may be words—of anger, perhaps, remorse, longing, loss. But these are words we can't easily express to other people. They come from deep within us and we need to have someone listen on that level. Animals can do that. They don't even have to tell us that they know how we feel. They simply do. And, in time, we feel well enough to savor life and to smile again.

SOUL MENDERS, one of the books in Guideposts' exclusive series, *LISTENING TO THE ANIMALS,* brings you true stories about the wonderful ways in which God's creatures minister to us in our times of need.

In our first chapter, *You're Special,* animals help us to overcome our self-doubt. Gary Shiebler, in "Sweet Kitty," recalls the little black cat who always seemed to know how to guide him through the ups and downs in the life of a young boy. "Working Overtime," by Thirza Peevey, is a delightful story about a crotchety old horse whose special fondness for his elderly owner gave her life meaning. "Spring Threshold," by Linda Johns, introduces us to two roosters who can teach us all a lot about devotion.

The stories in *I'm Right Here* brings us animals whose companionship and understanding heal our loneliness. Disney, a cat with a prickly personality, nevertheless proves to be the perfect friend for Toni Eames. In "Fine Feathered Friends," Gina Romsdahl relives her childhood days with her favorite playmate, a duck named (of course) Donald. Lorrie Kreigsch's cat teaches her that you don't have to be perfect to be loved.

In *Don't Be Afraid,* Lonnie Hull DuPont introduces us to a small black chicken whose affection and determination help her get through a severe depression. When Diane Ciarloni is nearly overcome by some difficult problems, a stray cat shows her the way back to prayer and trust in God.

Sometimes we help ourselves when we help each other. That's what happens in Gay Balliet's "Misty and His Guardian Angel," a touching story about a sick horse and the anxious little girl who loves him, in our fourth chapter, *Let Me Help You.* Then, when Nancy Gibbs is grieving over the loss of her father, she is comforted by the singing of birds coming from her father's hand-made bird houses. Leigh Singh, a young woman who has battled cerebral palsy since childhood, finds her hope renewed when a dog named Slugger leads her out into the world.

In our times of sadness—and we all have them—the stories in *Cheer Up!* will lead you back to joy. "Old Man Moreland" is a tender story about a duck named Ruby and a man with a mean streak. T. J. Banks tells us about a special cat whose understanding of her grief enabled her to come to terms with it. As a tribute to the remarkable power of animals to lift our spirits, even in the darkest hours, Gary Kowalski describes the annual Blessing of the Animals in his church.

We can learn so much from the animals in our lives. When our souls need mending, we can comfort each other by simply being there. We can listen with our hearts to what is said without words. We don't have to prove our love. We just have to live it.

PHYLLIS HOBE

SOUL
MENDERS

You're Special

*"The love for all living creatures is the
most noble attribute of man."*

CHARLES DARWIN

When I used to visit my dad in the nursing home where he lived for a few years, I often brought my dogs with me. Dad missed them and when he saw them his eyes lit up. And so did several of the other patients. Some of them simply didn't speak at all—not that they couldn't; they just didn't think anyone wanted to listen to them. But let one of my dogs walk up to them and look into their faces, and a conversation began. The patients would do the talking and the dog would listen.

Somehow the dogs were communicating something the doctors, nurses and other staff members weren't able to do. They let people know they were important.

Sweet Kitty

GARY SHIEBLER

When I was a boy, there were few things I loved more in the world than my blue Schwinn bicycle. Whether it be skimming through glassy puddles after a spring rain, soaring above sidewalk panels turned into launching ramps by swollen tree roots, or just riding up and down the driveway, she was my silver spoked magic carpet, my suburban steed. Above her sensible and sturdy frame, I tasted many of my first true moments of freedom, exhilaration and danger.

One of my favorite places to ride was right next door to my house. Bianchi's Wholesale Greenhouses was a mysterious, spooky place, a world filled with long shadows and peculiar sounds. A place where rows and rows of strange flowers bloomed beneath ghostly concourses of white-washed glass and chestnut-skinned men made fertilizer and sang songs under the hot August sun in languages I couldn't understand. A place of secret paths and alleys where a boy could ride his bicycle for as long as he wished. A place ripe with magic and filled with cats, secret cats that only came out at night. I used to watch them from my bedroom window, darting from behind tractors or scaling bales of peat in the light of the moon. I always hoped that one might be brave or curious enough to jump over the fence into our yard. One day, my wish came true.

"She must have come from Bianchi's," my mom remembers. "I found her out by the garage while I was hanging the laundry. It looked like her tail had been run over by a car or something. Took her up to the vet right away. We didn't have any choice but to keep her."

Mom said that about every stray that showed up in our yard. There was no such thing as the pound.

When asked about how they came up with Sweet Kitty's name, my mother's response is always the same.

"Talk to your father," she snaps.

Now, when it comes to naming cats, there's a bottomless well of exotic and unconventional names to choose from. In naming a dog, you have to be more practical. The simpler, more monosyllabic the name, the better and the more likely they are to understand commands and obey. Since cats rarely bother to listen to us at all, these rules to not apply, hence "Linford Bishop Rutherford III" is a totally acceptable name for a cat. It wouldn't, however, fly too well if you were trying to call your black lab home for dinner.

"She was sweet and she was a kitty," my father defends. This comes from the same man, who, when a gorgeous, black Persian wandered into our yard one November morning when I was twelve, lobbied for the name "New Black Kitty."

I'm glad mom had the final say in naming the kids.

Whether it be tending to the three litters of kittens she'd bear underneath my parents' bed or curling up next to the freshly clawed nose of our dog, Rusty, courtesy of an unprovoked encounter with her evil feline stepsister, Cokie, Sweet Kitty was the rock and ever nurturing mother cat of my childhood. Plump and portly, she was somewhere between a striped and spotted tabby and the loss of her tail only accentuated her rotund and matronly appearance. But she was built well, not easily ruffled, definitely more Butterfly McQueen than Vivian Leigh and her steady and calm demeanor seemed to soften the edges of our often frantic household.

Her coat was the typical tabby blend of blacks, browns and grays with ocelot-like spots running down her back and along her sides. These oblong markings conjoined at the top of her rump with a series of tigeresque stripes that spilled wildly down her ample flanks and thighs to sandy paws and dark feet. Her soft, gentle face was much too small for the large bouquet of whiskers that sprang from her ivory muzzle and her large, sharp ears completely dominated the top of her narrow head. Painted between those ears just above her brow, was a series of lines and stripes that formed the perfect letter "M", a fitting insignia for this grand matriarch.

We learned quickly that her defection from the field of glass was not a clean break, due in part to a big, black tom who usually held court at the base of the huge brick smoke-stack that helped heat the greenhouses in winter. For three successive springs, she'd disappear for a few days, only to grace us two months later, with a fresh quiver of newborns. Her delivery regime was always the same—each time she'd stroll belly-heavy into my parents' bedroom, usually just before they were getting ready to go out to dinner, let out a large meow, arch her back, disappear under the bed and emerge on the other side with a damp new arrival in her gentle mouth. Each brood was identical—one gray, one black, one tiger. Often in heels and stockings, my mother would hastily prepare the bottom drawer of my father's dresser, line it with towels and receiving blankets from when I was a baby, and for the next six weeks, the former outpost of my dad's pajamas would become a mewing nest of furry faces and hungry mouths.

Although my mom complained each time Sweet Kitty was pregnant, I could always detect a certain excitement and comfort in her eyes. And as much as I support the need for strict spay-and-neuter programs, I can't help but think that something's lost when we don't allow our children to experience at least one litter of kittens in their lifetimes. It's a precious process, to see a mother nurse her newborns, to watch eyes slowly open and personalities emerge. Each morning when I woke up, I couldn't wait to see the kittens, to hold my favorite one and hear their tiny mews. Even the process of finding them homes was a joy, as my mother hand-stenciled tiny birth certificates for each and made collars out of ribbon bearing colorful name tags. As a result, Sweet Kitty's kittens always got adopted and we received permanent imprints on our hearts as to the power of love, responsibility and importance of having cats in our lives at all times.

As soon as their eyes were fully open and legs not too wobbly, it was time to go to school. The middle of our kitchen floor was where Sweet Kitty taught her lessons and every morning after breakfast, she'd gather up her young pupils, march them to the front of the stove and lecture them on the finer points of stalking and hunting. On the days she decided to teach a lab, it was not unusual to find a live subject flapping and flailing about the linoleum floor. With all three litters, she was strict and extremely committed to her curriculum. One might imagine her teaching schedule looking something like this:

Mondays and Wednesdays 8-10 am "Fundamentals of Mousing"
Tuesdays 1-3 pm "Bird Feeders: A Cat's Best Friend"

Thursdays 9-11 am "Moles, Voles, Chipmunks and You"
Fridays 8-10 am "How to Walk Past Cokie, the Meanest Cat
in the World, Without Losing an Eye."

When classes were over, mom would play janitor to Sweet Kitty's graphic presentations and dutifully clean up the smorgasbord of feathers, spleens and fur scattered beneath cabinets and under barstools. One morning, she made the mistake of carrying an overflowing laundry basket through the kitchen in her bare feet without watching where she was going. Suddenly, she felt something warm and gushy rise up between her toes. Tossing the basket aside, she looked down and much to her horror, saw the pancaked remains of a rabbit head.

Probably one of Sweet Kitty's evening classes.

Although she was gracious and kind to us all, there was never any doubt that Sweet Kitty was my mother's cat. They seemed to share a deep and common bond, a maternal understanding that there was no greater purpose in life than staying close to home and raising a family. And when my mom and dad's marriage was on the brink of falling apart when I was a teenager, it was Sweet Kitty that helped my mother through the longest nights and hours of despair. I'd often see them sitting together in the rocker by the fireplace after a particularly harsh fight, my mom lost in a tearful gaze. It was a sad, yet strangely reassuring sight, for it left a permanent impression as to how important our cats can be, particularly when we've been hurt or betrayed by our own kind. And while I'm not sure what role Sweet Kitty played in saving my parents' marriage, (they'll be celebrating their fiftieth anniversary next month) I'm confident of one thing. She was one of the few things my mom could depend on in a time when most things were falling apart.

When Sweet Kitty was twelve, she was diagnosed with cancer. Despite her age and the fact that my folks had little money, there was never any question about what needed to be done. She was family, an immeasurable part of our daily existence and my parents vowed to do anything to save her.

The operation was a success, but it cost her the use of her left front leg. Over time, she learned to compensate for the loss. I'll never forget how bravely and determinedly she'd struggle up into laps or hobble down stairwells, as if to demonstrate her gratitude for getting a second chance. And although it was uncomfortable and awkward, particularly in the beginning, the cast that she had to wear on her leg for the first few months proved to be the perfect solution to Cokie's sneak attacks.

"She'd just turn around and club her over the head," mom remembers. "She never bothered her again."

It's easy to appreciate the value of a dog that greets a young boy on a front lawn after school, bounding, tail wagging, tongue dangling, eyes beaming. It's not as easy to mark the importance of a sleeping cat curled up on a cobbler's bench next to where you drop your book bag every day. If Rusty was the perfect dog and angel of my childhood, Sweet Kitty was my trusted anchor. Her simple and steady presence helped me believe, even in the most uncertain times, that everything was going to be all right. And while most of my memories of her have faded into a blurry tapestry of snapshots and lore, reminiscences of a life that surrounded her remain vivid. An old German clock ticks softly on the living room mantle. A Nat King Cole record spins softly inside a wooden console. An orange moon slowly rises in the eastern sky above a great smokestack.

I want to go back to that small house next to the field of glass.

I want to stand on frosty steps in my pajamas and call her name just like my father used to do.

"Sweeeet Kitty . . . Sweeeet Kitty. . . . "

I want to see her bound up out of the darkness and disappear between my slippered feet into the house. I want to pick her up, feel her weight in my arms, explore her coat with my fingers. I want to stop for a moment, look into her eyes, catalog her meow, memorize her purr. I want to tell her about a boy's life, those barreling, leaping, tumbling days that tatter the knees of blue jeans and scrape elbows. A boy's life, where everything moves so fast and playing king of the hill and wrestling with dogs reign supreme. A life of taking things for granted, of racing in and out of doors, of riding bicycles and running past things.

A boy's life.

from A SEARCH FOR THE PERFECT CAT

Her Own Song

MARY ALICE BAUMGARDNER

Sometimes God's messengers present themselves in the most mundane places, at the very moment when we especially need some reassurance of His Love.

A number of years ago, on a bleak January morning, a manuscript was returned to me. I had had such high hopes that this particular publisher would be "the" one. A form rejection letter advised me otherwise. My spirits plunged, matching that icy, gray day. I felt so discouraged, so unappreciated, so unloved.

"I'm just making a fool of myself," I murmured. "Why do I keep on trying to get my stories published? I should just quit... and do something else."

I wondered what else I could do. The children's stories I wrote seemed to tumble into my heart, demanding to be written. I believed in the messages in them. I believed that, in some way, they could encourage youngsters. Within humorous situations they told about persevering, overcoming obstacles, appreciating the uniqueness of one's self and celebrating the differences in others. Oh, I had written lots of stories!

Parents, educators, librarians and the kids themselves assured me they related to my stories. No, they weren't preachy, they were fun. They were true. And yet, none of my stories had found a home.

Standing at the kitchen window, still holding onto the "bad news," I looked outside. Tears blurred my vision, but I could see a little bird on the feeder. I heard her chirp and watched as she continued to dine. Suddenly she lifted off in the direction of the woods.

I thought about that little bird, going into the woods alone. I thought about her singing . . . singing whether anyone hears her or not. Of course, she sings! She sings because she has a song!

It was then I discovered that I write because I, too, have a "song": a story. I realized that I will keep writing as long as I have a story. And I will keep on writing whether or not anyone else hears my song.

Very gently the question came to me: "Who gave you your song, Mary Alice?"

Yes, it was with humility and gratitude that I whispered, "Thank you, dear Lord." He has, indeed, given each of us different gifts, special talents, a "song to sing." And how delightful that a little bird should tell me so!

Love for Sale

NANCY B. GIBBS

We've all heard it said that you can't buy love. A little over nine years ago, I proved that statement wrong. In addition, I bought love at a discounted price.

From the time I was a small child, I wanted a toy poodle. I thought it would be grand to have a dog with bows in her hair and painted toenails. I pictured myself walking my poodle down the street with her head held high. Over the years, I had big dogs, mixed breeds and scruffy dogs, but I never owned a poodle.

After I married, I continued to beg for a poodle. "We don't need any sissy dogs around here," my husband said. I realized that he was right. The last thing we needed was another mouth to feed. We already had two cats, two dogs and three kids.

One winter morning, however, I opened the newspaper. "Toy poodles for sale," the advertisement read. The words jumped out at me instantly. I picked up the telephone and, without thinking, dialed the number. It rang once, then twice, and I started to hang up.

"Hello," I faintly heard.

"I'm calling about your ad in the classified section," I blurted out.

"Oh, yes," the lady said. "I have two puppies left. They're adorable."

"I'll be there during my lunch break. Will you hold one for me?" I asked.

"Sure, I will," she said.

When I walked up to the door, a lady met me with a puppy in each arm. The puppy in her left arm was squirming, wiggling and barking. The smaller puppy sat very still in her right arm. The squirming puppy looked very healthy. The quiet puppy's eyes were runny and she didn't make a sound. She didn't take her eyes off me, however. I saw love in those big brown eyes.

"I'll give you this one at a discount price," the lady said, holding out the puppy in her right arm. "She doesn't seem very healthy or active, but the vet says she's fine."

"I'll take her," I said. "She's the one I want." I reached out and took the quiet little puppy in my arms. "I've always loved the runt of the litter."

"Are you sure?" the lady asked. "I thought you would want this active pup—the one with personality."

"Oh no," I said, "this one has a great personality."

That night I took my newest baby home. She cuddled up close to me. I slept sitting up, holding my toy poodle, Daisey Doodle. We were both very content just to be together.

Two days later, I became very ill and emergency surgery was required. During the next few weeks, Daisey stayed right with me. I taught her many tricks while I was home with her. Even though she was a tiny ball of fur, she learned to dance, to sit up and to give me five. She learned to beg and even how to pat-a-cake. My recovery time sped by while we played together.

Since then, Daisey has been my best friend. She's right beside me with every step I take. When I sit down, she's in my lap. She plays computer with me and barks at the screen saver.

She loves me almost as much as I love her. She wears fancy bows in her hair and her toenails are painted to match her bows.

Whoever came up with the idea that you can't buy love hasn't ever met Daisey. The lady's advertisement read, "Poodles for Sale," but I know it should have read, "Love for Sale."

My dream of having a toy poodle finally came true. Daisey was definitely worth the wait. She is also worth much more than I paid for her. I not only bought a puppy; I bought a friend, a companion and a great deal of love. I got a great bargain when I bought the sissy dog, which I really didn't need, but wanted desperately.

Mama Cat

LYNN SEELY

When I was almost four years old I was a mere bit of a girl. Curly hair framed my happy little freckled face and my lively blue eyes looked at everything in curious anticipation of delights yet to be. One beautiful September day my mother stretched out on the sofa and called to me. She asked me to bring her a cool, wet cloth for her forehead. She said she had a headache. I was happy to do such a grown-up thing and felt very important as I brought her the cloth. That done, I then skipped outside to play in my yard.

I never saw my mother again. She died of polio three days later, just one week before I turned four years old. The loss was total, irreversible and devastating. And I could not change it. No matter how I cried. No matter how good I promised to be. No matter how many threats I issued. No matter how desperately I wanted her back. My mother was gone, never to return to me. Never again to hug me close, or brush my hair, or tuck me in bed, or sing softly to me as I drifted off to sleep in perfect peace. Nor would she ever again gaze at me with love. And tragically, all too soon after she died, she began to fade from my memory. It was difficult to remember what her face looked like, or remember the tender gaze that always transmitted how much she loved me.

I was tormented by the idea that perhaps my mother left me because I was bad. I couldn't remember what I had done, but I must have done something to cause her to leave. That burden weighed heavily on my heart. There was no peace for me. Only dreadful longing and unutterable guilt.

Soon after her death, while trees were still dressed in scarlet and gold—before the leaves had floated to the ground and left limbs bare—I overheard the mailman speak to a neighbor. He called out as he passed her home, "Those are sure cute kittens." Although I had been withdrawn and listless, the idea of seeing kittens drew me to the neighbor's home. I avoided being seen by anyone as I entered the backyard. There, in a wooden tool shed was a box that held a beautiful white cat who had recently given birth to kittens. She was tucked away in the corner of the neat, dry shed. It was a cozy place.

The mother cat snuggled close to her babies. It suddenly reminded me of the times I had snuggled close to my own mother, and the grief that had engulfed my heart began to ease a little. I wanted my mother, but I could not have her anymore. After a few minutes, my four-year-old mind came up with a simple plan. I would become a kitten. And this beautiful mother cat would be my second mama. And since she was a mother herself, I reasoned, I could talk to her about my own mother. I knew she would understand. The mama cat's eyes seemed to transmit the sweetest love to her kittens and reminded me of the special loving look in my own mother's eyes. For the first time since my mother died, I smiled.

Each day I would visit Mama Cat. She liked being gently stroked by my little hands. Her fur was silky and soft and somehow comforting to me. Mama Cat purred loudly and talked to her babies in soft meows. She began to include me in her circle of love, too. She would gaze at me and purr loudly whenever I was near. I knew what she was saying—a four-year-old just knows these things. She was saying, "I love you, my babies," and I knew she included me, too.

I talked to her about my mother and how much I missed her. Mama Cat always seemed to understand. I couldn't speak to anyone else about the confusing, jumbled-up pain that was in my heart, but I could talk to Mama Cat. She always listened patiently and she seemed to be very wise. My heart began to heal during the days that followed as Mama Cat showed me how much she loved all of us. I was absolutely certain that when I was with my Mama Cat I was a kitten. I believed if someone were to glance into the tool shed, they would not see a child, they would see me as a kitten—so powerful was my imagination as a four-year-old.

As time passed and the kittens grew bigger, they no longer listened to the mother cat as well as they should have. They would ignore her worried meows to behave and stay close— they would race in and out of the tool shed and even climb way up a tree. I could always tell when Mama Cat was worried. My own mother used to get the same worried look when I would climb too high on my swing set after being told not to. She would rush over, lift me down, and chide me for not listening to her. Then she would kiss me, smile and extract a promise that I would be more careful—though the following day I would be back up on the top of the swing set again. In watching how much Mama Cat loved her misbehaving kittens, I came to understand the profound truth that my mother didn't leave me because I was bad, nor had she stopped loving me when I disobeyed her. Knowing that eased the ache in my heart.

For one very special season, I took refuge in the innocent land of make believe within my young mind. I was one of the kittens this mother cat loved. That Mama Cat loved me was certain. That she eased a profound loss was also true. And her tender acceptance of me helped me fix the memory of my mother in my mind forever. When Mama Cat would snuggle against me and comfort me, it was always a reminder of when I had snuggled in my mother's arms. Mama Cat was always glad to see me, just as my real mother had been. She would gaze at me with love, as my real mother had done. No one else looked at me that way anymore. No one else was glad to see me. No one else worried about me, yet Mama Cat did. She helped me keep the sweetest memories of my real mother from fading.

Many years later I became a mother. When my son was an infant I would hold him in my arms and gaze at him with tenderness. As he grew older, each year brought more delight, and my heart would fill with love. And sometimes my heart would wander back to the tender memory of my own mother's love—and to a Mama Cat that helped a lonely, motherless waif of a girl come to terms with loss. In my mind, even now, I can still see the face of my own mother and her tender loving gaze. And I can still see the sweet, loving acceptance in the eyes of Mama Cat.

Working Overtime

THIRZA PEEVEY

I have often been amazed that many people with substantial orthopedic disabilities are able to ride horses independently, even without any training. It seems that horses are such sensitive creatures that they are often able to perceive the problem with little or no special training. At one stable where I worked for nine months, we had four different people with four very different horses who rode without any assistance. Two of them went hunting and rode over fences. Most of the horses were very sweet-natured and maternal mares, but one was a grumpy old man of a gelding.

One mare had learned to compensate for a rider with only one hand by neck reining and turning to leg pressure and weight. She was a fine-spirited mare who loved to run to the hounds, but she was wonderfully obedient to her mistress's hand. Another elderly woman had a wonderfully gentle old Quarter-Horse mare that also took great care of her.

One of my favorite mares in the string of six horses I cared for was a lovely bay mare of undetermined ancestry named Fortuna. I tried not to play favorites among my horses, but rather gave each the same high-quality care and affection that I gave every other. Fortuna was different, however. I couldn't help but love her. Fortuna made it her life's work to give her mistress, "Mrs. F," a safe and enjoyable trip every time. Mrs. F was an older woman with sparkling eyes and a very kind nature. She loved Fortuna very dearly and had been riding and hunting her for years. A few years previously, Mrs. F's arthritic hips had required replacement. For many people, this would have been the end of their days in the saddle, but Mrs. F continued riding. Fortuna generously braced herself and stood like a rock while Mrs. F levered herself painfully into the saddle. Once she was mounted, they were off for another exciting day of adventure.

I never understood how Mrs. F could bear the lateral movements of riding. With painful hips, it is very difficult to stay in the saddle if the horse moves sideways or if you get off balance. In the middle of that winter, we had several days when the ice crusting was so bad that the horses couldn't go outside to exercise in the pastures. Every available groom was pressed into service to exercise the horses in the oval-shaped barn aisle. I am not a very good rider, due to my own bad hip, so I was assigned to ride Fortuna and pony an equally gentle mare. That was how I discovered Mrs. F's secret. Fortuna had learned to balance a rider the way that one might vertically balance a pencil on the end of one's finger. If I became unbalanced to one side or the other, she simple stepped under me. Fortuna had learned to compensate for Mrs. F's weakness and had generously applied that knowledge to me.

Another horse and I didn't have quite the same relationship. Overtime was aptly named, as he was nearly thirty and still working. He was a crotchety old man who seemed to enjoy his misery and that of anyone around him that he could infect. Not only was he bad tempered, he was homely too. He looked rather like he had been put together by committee.

He was a Quarter Horse, but parts of him looked Morgan or Walking Horse. On top of that, he was a kicker. According to a friend who had known the horse since he was a three-year-old, he had always kicked and consequently he had always had thrush.

Thrush is normally a nuisance problem. Horses' feet are designed for life on a dry savanna, but humans insist on keeping them in damp stalls and muddy paddocks. In damp conditions the soft stretchy frog gets infected with fungus. The frog is meant to serve as a shock absorber, allowing the heels to spread and dissipate shock as the foot strikes the ground. As the foot leaves the ground, the frog contracts, sending blood back toward the heart and preparing the foot to act as a spring when it next strikes the ground. If the frog becomes diseased, the shock absorber stops working, sending several thousand pounds of force up the leg each time the foot hits the ground. Most of the time, picking the feet daily and painting the frog with bleach, iodine or a commercial preparation if it stinks or turns black and gooey is enough to keep it healthy. Left to its own devices it can become entrenched.

In OT's case, his kicking had kept his caretakers from treating his foot for so long that the frog in his right hind had been eaten away. That foot had contracted to about two-thirds its normal size. Not only was he sending shock waves through his body with every step, but also the fragile laminae and coffin bone inside his foot were protected only by a smooth thin callus.

When he was assigned to me, my boss also warned me about his temper, his kicking and his thrush. "I put a squeeze bottle in your grooming box. There is a mixture of formaldehyde, glycerin and iodine in it that the vet made up for him. It's extra strong stuff, since you'll only be able to get it in his feet when he is willing. It has to get into his feet at least three times a week. Don't get it in your eyes and don't get hurt."

The other grooms warned me about his owner. According to them, she was more than a bit eccentric. "She always wears a helmet. It never comes off her head. She goes out in the back pasture with him and sleeps on his back. You'll have a hard time not laughing. Make sure you don't—there is no quicker way to get in trouble."

A few days after Overtime was assigned to me, I stayed late to take care of some returning hunters. OT's owner showed up an hour before I left. She drove into the driveway already wearing her riding helmet, as the others had said. I soon saw why. She was so elderly and unstable on her feet that no sooner did she get out of the car than she fell on her head. She wasn't hurt, and she didn't let it bother her. She got up, brushed off my help, dusted herself off and went to the tack room to get her saddle and bridle. She got a grooming box out of her car and took it to OT's stall where she groomed him from head to toe. She picked his feet and painted them. I had already done all that an hour before; she was just enjoying his company.

A half-hour later, I opened the gate for her as she headed into the back field. I watched from the fence as she immediately fell asleep on his back. OT grazed quietly, stepping under her as she slid from side to side, just like Fortuna did for Mrs. F. Eventually the time came when he wasn't quick enough to catch her—he was nearly thirty after all—and she slid to the ground. She was so relaxed and asleep that she wasn't hurt, it just woke her up. Then she dusted herself off, climbed back on and went back to sleep.

I walked away from the gate with a new view of Overtime. I saw that even though he was ugly and cranky to everyone else in the world, he loved his mistress, and in her eyes he was beautiful. I realized that riding the old horse gave his owner a reason to be out and about in the beautiful countryside while most folks of her age and physical condition rarely got out of the house. Many of them were probably in nursing homes. Because of that cranky old Walter Matthau of a horse, she still drove a car, she still got regular exercise and she still enjoyed life. I also realized that when OT's time came, it would probably end her riding. No young horse would have the history and relationship with her to protect her the way OT did. I knew then that the old horse was precious beyond words. The thrush would stop with me, no matter how much work it took. Even more so, the kicking would stop with me. I didn't want to get him healthy only to have it come back when I left because he still scared every caretaker he had.

The next day, I put OT in cross ties. I took my time brushing him, scratching all his itchy spots and massaging sore spots until he was relaxed and dozing. I did his front feet next, as he didn't mind them. When I asked for his left hind, he drew back and fired. I was ready for him and I dodged sideways as the foot whistled harmlessly past me. Before he could get balanced, I yelled "No!" and fired, kicking him in the tush with the flat side of my foot. I didn't want to hurt him, just startle him and make a point.

In a herd, the stallion is the protector, not the leader. The leader is usually a middle-aged mare who has been around some time, but is still young enough to discipline the others. She rules by warning first with a squeal, a pinned ear, a glare, bared teeth, or a cocked hind foot. If the others don't obey, she kicks. Usually, she hits the other horse in the belly or the muscle of the hindquarter with sufficient force to sting and make a loud noise. Rarely does she hurt them. After a few swats like that, all she needs is the warning. I was attempting to mimic this natural behavior as closely as I could.

The kick worked. OT was startled and leaped as far forward as the cross ties allowed. Then he turned sideways where he could see me and rolled his eyes and snorted. I had made my point and had gotten his attention and respect. Now I had to keep it.

I approached him, crooning soothingly and started all over. I straightened him up in the cross ties and stroked him until he relaxed again. Then I asked for his foot again, running my hand down his leg and tapping him gently under the fetlock. Instantly, he fired again. I was still on my guard, and the kick whistled by harmlessly again. Again I shouted "No!" and booted him in the tush. His response was the same as before. The third time I asked, he bore down on the foot and refused to move. I tugged on the hair of his fetlock with no success. I squeezed his tendons to no avail. Finally, I pressed the hoof pick against his fetlock. He fired again, with the same consequences.

On the fourth try, he offered his foot like a gentleman and stood while I cleaned his foot and treated it. I had to repeat the lesson on the right hind, but it only took one round. We were making progress.

Over the next week, we consistently fought every night. However, I made sure that I won each time. I didn't give up until he had stood like a gentleman for me to treat both hind feet. By the second week, he offered his foot nicely and stood quietly most nights. Occasionally, he tried to kick just to see if I was paying attention. I always was. The next time the blacksmith came, he pronounced OT thrush-free. At the end of three months, OT had tissue growing where the frog should be. It wasn't really a frog, but it was healthy and clean. The best part was, he didn't kick anymore. When I moved on, I left with a clear conscience. I knew that the next groom wouldn't have any trouble taking care of OT's feet and that I had done my best to ensure that OT could continue to give his owner something to look forward to for as long as possible.

When I left that job to move back to Kentucky, I kept in touch with the people I had worked with for several years. I learned from them that OT had had only a few more years after I left. I'm sure his owner is gone by now, too. However, I learned a few things from them. Just because a horse is old doesn't mean his usefulness is done. Old horses can give old people joy and something to look forward to. It isn't only the sweet horses, like Fortuna, who give love and sacrifice to their owners.

It is just short of a cruelty not to train a young horse how to behave. Bad behavior can make it nearly impossible to give the animal good care. And finally, even if a horse is old it is worth retraining him. Retraining the horse makes it possible to take proper care of him. Sort of like removing a thorn from a lion's paw.

Oh, and incidentally, I learned to love the old horse, too.

Back to School

MARY M. ALWARD

It was love at first sight. The adorable Alaskan Malamute pup lay on his mistress's lap, tail wagging, not moving a muscle. His eyes, one blue and one brown, lit up at the sight of my grandsons. His tail thumped a staccato on the vinyl seat.

We had seen an ad for the pup in the local newspaper. Because his owner lived so far out of town, he offered to bring the pup to our home so we could see him. The boys loved him and my husband took an immediate liking to this gray-and-white dog with a black back. My husband nodded at me. "We'll take him," we told the man and his wife.

Once the pup was in the house, we decided he needed a name. The day before I had made a list of acceptable names so the boys could do the actual choosing. I had researched Eskimo names on the Internet and came up with Mikolak (pronounced Me-ko-lack). The name meant "small one with a big heart." The other choices were Phantom and Shadow. The pup was quiet and gentle. Everyone agreed that Mikolak fit his personality perfectly.

Before the day was over, the grandsons had decided the pup needed a nickname. Brandon, the oldest, suggested Meeko, for short. Meeko was the mischievous raccoon from the *Pocahontas* movie. So Meeko it was.

For the first few days, Meeko was quiet. We hardly knew he was in the house. As he became more familiar with his surroundings and us, he began to live up to his name. He always seemed to be into some kind of mischief.

As Meeko grew, I began to suspect he was going to surpass the sixty-five pounds that his owner had told us he would be as an adult. This dog was going to be gigantic! The vet confirmed this when I took him for his first shot. "Probably about one hundred to one hundred twenty pounds," he said. "But he's a keeper. I've never seen an Alaskan Malamute with such a gentle and quiet disposition."

Because he was going to be such a large dog, my husband and I decided he needed to go to obedience school—or, rather, we did, in order to control this energetic ball of fur that was going to stand as high as our hips in adulthood. After all, living in the city provided ample opportunity for disaster if he didn't obey our every command.

We checked several obedience schools in our area and decided to go with the one that the vet recommended, even though it was a little more expensive. They had a great success rate and had been in business for many years. Their Head Start Program taught basic control skills to us humans and socialization skills to the canines.

Meeko was the largest breed in the class of ten dogs. In the beginning, he decided he didn't want anything to do with this social program. The first time we allowed him off his lead to play with the other pups, he was very defensive. When the tiny pups approached him, he barked furiously, backed into a corner and raised his hackles, warning them to keep their distance. When they continued their approach, he cowered and crawled under a bench.

We all laughed heartily. What a sight to see a 25-pound dog hiding from a boxer that was less than half his weight. He was the star of the show. Even the trainer got a good chuckle when she saw that Meeko was scared to death of a dog that weighed only about nine pounds.

The second week of class, Meeko had learned to sit, shake-a-paw and follow basic hand signals as long as those hands held a tasty treat. He was a little more sociable but spent most of playtime hiding under a bench. Though he had grown, most of the other pups hadn't. We wondered if he would always be somewhat antisocial, but the trainer assured us he would "come around."

During the next week I spent a lot of time training Meeko. Our grandsons visited twice that week and had soon coaxed Meeko out of his shell. The third week of class, he proved to be quite a different pup. When playtime came, he joined in, romping and running with the other pups. He now weighed thirty-two pounds and it was hilarious to see him back away from the smaller dogs when they became overly aggressive.

We missed the fourth and last week of class due to a very heavy snowfall that dumped three feet of snow in our area. Meeko will still receive his diploma and we continue to work with him on a daily basis. At sixteen weeks, he now weighs fifty-five pounds and has learned his lessons fairly well. He lies quietly while we eat, not begging or whining. He fetches a ball, spends hours playing with his favorite toys and loves to go for a walk at least twice a day. However, he is weak in two areas: he doesn't always come when called, which could put him in a dangerous situation in a busy city, and he hates the "down" command. In fact, there are times when he refuses to lie down unless a tasty treat is used to bribe him.

Meeko is growing up. He only nips on occasion, and when he wants attention, he lifts his large paw and rests it on a knee. He loves to run and play with our grandsons and, just like any youngster of the animal kingdom, he loves life and lives it to the fullest.

But we humans still need a few lessons on how to control such a large dog. So, for Meeko's sake and ours, it is back to obedience school next month. I'm looking forward to it.

Spring Threshold

LINDA JOHNS

The thermometer veered yet again.

With the seasons between winter and spring, the fickle weather produced neither snow nor warmth but drizzled freezing rain for days.

Ice coated all the tree buds, staple food for ruffed grouse. Ice hardened almost immediately on birdseed scattered over the ground. Ice crusted the woodlands, creating treacherous walking for deer already wearied by winter's vagaries.

And ice continually re-formed on walkways or car windows, inspiring new levels of profanity in certain humans—humans, like deer, wearied by winter's vagaries.

Finally one morning, the cloudbank oozed moodily into the northeast to brighten other lives with its dreary dripping. Sunshine burst over the land, vanquishing the gloom and igniting the silvered trees in eye-dazzling glory. Tiny rainbows sprang into being out of prismatic glitter. The icy coating of branches surrendered to the warmth and broke away, falling in musical tinklings on the crust below the trees. Brooks danced.

After the long silence of winter, we could hear nature's pulse beating again.

The very earth seemed to sigh and relax.

From the roof one evening, Mack and I watched deer venturing out into the meadow. A crow passed, bearing a large twig for nest-building. Below us, five skunks emerged from under the studio, their usual winter quarters. They congregated under the feeders and began searching for food.

Of one accord, we began tossing pieces of cookie among them, giggling helplessly at their varied reactions as cookies rained down out of the sky.

I tried to toss my offerings in front of each skunk. If I succeeded, the skunk immediately cornered the morsel and began to eat. If my aim was off, I usually struck a skunk on the head. He'd jump back, blundering into one of his companions, and tails, like questions, would be raised.

Mack, with his usual trickster humour, aimed only for the skunks. Whenever a fragment bounced off a skunk's back, the victim would instantly erect an outraged tail and glare around at the others. They, oblivious of any broken taboos, would continue to chew blissfully. The smitten skunk, realizing he would miss his share, would then lower his tail—but only gradually, as though not entirely convinced that he hadn't been insulted. He, too, would be blissfully chewing when the next chunk struck him.

One of the skunks was an old favourite named Sooty. Only the top of her head and the tip of her tail were white. The long stripe joining them was missing, and her back was black. Seen from above in the deepening dusk, Sooty in motion looked like one small white creature chasing another—or two romping in tandom.

Indoors, spring's energy was affecting the roosters. Very little dirt remained in the large box that I had provided for indoor dustbaths. They were eager to luxuriate in sun-warmed earth and scratch up feasts of bugs. Unfortunately, though mild winds teased the land and southern slopes were beginning to respond, ice still prevailed, and the ground remained frozen. Bubble began to get edgy. Occasional pseudo-cockfights became tainted with serious undertones.

We came home one day to a crisis.

The boys had had a disagreement, and Squeak, the smaller of the two, was injured. Over the previous couple of years, a peculiar lump had developed on his magnificent comb. This lump had now been punctured and was bleeding profusely. Blood trickled down the side of Squeak's face, and he shook his head repeatedly, splattering gore all over the studio. His chest plumage was saturated.

The fight had probably been no worse than their usual brief encounters, because the boys were now cozied down together. If the lump hadn't been punctured, the situation wouldn't have been serious.

For two hours we laboured to stop the bleeding. We tried direct pressure, antibiotic ointment, and finally unbleached flour. The lump persistently refilled and dripped blood. Flour proved to be the most effective, but every handful also dusted the bloody plumage on his chest, forming a revolting paste.

After the bleeding had stopped for half an hour, it began again. I quickly coated an adhesive bandage with antibiotic ointment and folded it around the comb, pressing it down thoroughly. The flow finally ceased.

We washed Squeak's plumage, marvelling at his patient, trusting nature, and dried him with a blow-dryer. Then I fastened a sock over his foot to prevent him scratching his comb. With lots of reassuring hugs, we bedded him down.

Bubble we also fitted out with socks in case he caused further complications and, for the first time in their lives, separated the boys for the night. An hour's scrubbing restored the studio, and we reeled off to bed ourselves, bone-deep exhausted.

Five days later I removed Squeak's bandage, which was hanging off his comb. The cut looked sealed, but in fifteen minutes began bleeding again. Though Mack and I laboured for an hour and a half with flour and corn starch, applying direct pressure, pressure above, and adhesive bandages, we couldn't stop the bleeding. Professional help was needed. Despite Bubble's shrill cries, we bundled up Squeak, carried him out to the car, and drove rapidly to town.

He lay trustfully in my arms while I caressed his neck feathers and reassured him. But his utter passivity chilled my heart.

The vet tried repeatedly to tie off the bleeding with a stitch. Then he opened the lump further, seeking for another bleeder. He cauterized twice.

Nothing worked.

Finally he decided to put Squeak under a general anesthetic and add stitches to permanently deflate the lump. To stop what he called the aneurysm.

I still held Squeak in my arms. The mask was fitted over his face, and he sank into unconsciousness. I remained holding him, trying to convey reassurance. Trying to hold onto his life.

But in vain.

In a few minutes, Squeak stopped breathing. Never a strong chicken, he'd lost too much blood to be able to withstand the added burden of the anesthetic. Devastated, I carried him home and froze his body for burial in the spring.

Numbed with grief, I stumbled out to the studio to see Bubbs. He welcomed me in his usual way, picking up tidbits and laying them at my feet, but I couldn't respond. I remained silent, sickened, leaning against the doorway. Finally I slid down onto my knees, staring wordlessly at him.

Bubble froze. He stared intently into my eyes. For several long moments, he remained utterly motionless, not even blinking, while I told him about Squeak. Our interlocked gaze created a bridge of communication that was almost palpable. Almost visible.

I had absolutely no doubt that Bubble understood my message. He knew now that Squeak was dead. He walked silently into my arms, and we hugged long and hard.

Outside the window, snow began to fall. Large, soft flakes like feathers. No two alike. I used to describe Squeak's tweedy white plumage as snowflake plumage. No two of his feathers were ever patterned alike.

That night, in the living room, Bubbs jumped up onto my legs and, after we hugged, lay down across my knees. He left my lap bare, as though an invisible Squeak lay in his usual spot.

Maybe he did.

Over the next few weeks, I tried to comfort Bubble, to ease his obvious despondency. I coaxed him to eat his usual favourite foods, but he grieved, and food had little interest for him. He hated to eat alone and ate very little if we chanced to be away during the day. Often I brought his dish into the living room in the evenings and watched sadly as he happily ate the same food he'd left all day. He showed an accelerated interest in sharing my food instead, and ate very tidily off my plate. New foods became his favourites—stewed rhubarb and strawberries; cooked green or yellow beans, which he swallowed whole like a human sucking back a strand of spaghetti; peanut butter and honey on bread; cooked squash and carrots; scalloped potatoes; stir-fried veggies; pita-bread veggie sandwiches.

With Squeak gone he seemed to identify wholly with us, and we often took him along in the car. He rode like a king in my lap.

I wondered if he saw Squeak everywhere, as I did. And heard him. Heard Squeak's deep clucks of joy when lettuce, raisins, or warm macaroni arrived in the morning food dish. Heard his piercing crows prodding the sun to be up and doing.

Saw him standing beside me as I painted, tugging on my pantleg so I'd caress his neck feathers with my free hand. Saw his smug contentment as he sat in my lap before the easel. Saw him asleep in my arms, snoring trustfully.

Whenever both roosters were snuggled down in my lap, Squeak had liked to curl his toes up in the palm of my hand. As they warmed, he'd doze blissfully—a ritual that stemmed from his chick days, when his whole body could lie basking in the warmth of my hand. He was sensitive to chilling.

Squeak was still everywhere. Watching Mack play guitar or bake bread. Letting fledgling birds sit on his back. Lifting his wings to me in his own special greeting.

His patience with his own problems was enviable. He had staggered about gallantly in homemade shoes as a chick to straighten his toes. His coordination lingered long behind Bubble's, so that even his ability to jump into my lap was achieved months later than Bubbs'. One wing was permanently twisted, and often hurt him when it was touched. He had chronic ear problems, which meant I had to clean his ears every week. Even his beautiful plumage took months to first develop, rather than a few weeks.

Squeak definitely had "special needs."

I'll always be grateful to that thin plumage that decreed

that Squeak would never survive outdoor winters in sheds as do other chickens. Living with both roosters indoors involved me in a rich companionship I would otherwise have missed.

It filled my days with fascinating insights. Provided me with interaction at depths never known to someone who approaches chickens only to feed or to pen them.

I have been privileged.

       from A FEATHERED FAMILY

Small Miracles

LONNIE HULL DuPONT

One chilly March evening, my husband Joe and I were getting ready to settle in for the night when we heard a little cry outside. Although we live in a fairly remote area, we are on a state road that has a fair number of big trucks. To hear such a small cry was unusual.

It got louder and more insistent. I looked out the front door, and there, sitting in a pool of light from our window, sat the homeliest little half-kitten/half-cat. She was all mouth, looking me right in the eye, crying for something to eat. She was around six months old, scrawny and missing some teeth, and, boy, was she loud!

"What should we do?" my husband said.

"Well, we have to feed her out back," I said. "We can't let her go hungry." I thought for a moment and added, "And you have to do it. I'll get attached, and she's just going to get run over by a truck. You have to feed her."

My husband nodded. "I'm allergic to cats, so you know I won't get attached."

Famous last words. When Joe came in later, he was visibly moved. "She drooled right on the ground, she was so hungry," he reported. "But she rubbed and rubbed on me first, as if she were thanking me."

Joe fed her out by the barn for the next several weeks. My husband's allergies kept us from letting her in, but she seemed not to want to come inside anyway. She was skittish and seemed to like being outside as long as she was fed. She was clearly taking care of herself, not being hounded by the wild animals around here. Spring came early and warm that year, so life wasn't too bad for the cat.

What Joe hadn't told me was that he and the cat were bonding. He would tap a can against the barn and she'd sashay her way to him, then rub on him. He'd pick her up, place her forehead against his, and they would just be that way for awhile. Then he'd put her by her food where she hunkered down and ate. All the time she ate, Joe would pet her back really hard. She loved it. I think it made her feel safe, and in a primitive way, she had another creature literally to watch her back while she ate in the wild.

But we knew our place was dangerous. Strays never seemed to survive the truck traffic. And though it was spring, we knew winter in Michigan is no place for outdoor cats. We had no shelter for her—the barn was not ours and was locked up. We couldn't let her in the house because of Joe's allergy—he always had allergy attacks at houses with pet cats.

My brother-in-law offered to take her for his barn. He had a long-horn steer ranch and could use a mouser. That wouldn't be a bad life for a cat who seemed to like the outdoors—she'd have plenty of warm hay to sleep in and daily human interaction. So one night we put the cat in a travel box and drove the eight miles to the ranch. She cried most of the way, and we talked soothingly to her. At the ranch, she was unnerved, but eventually she sat down and ate, then began grooming. We left.

But I was in tears. I felt we'd abandoned an animal that

had clearly been abandoned once before. Joe reminded me that we were trying to help a scrappy little cat survive, that it really was a good thing. I felt sick to my stomach about leaving her, but I had to agree.

Ten nights later, Joe walked by the front door and glanced out. There in a pool of light sat the cat, looking him straight in the eye, this time quietly.

"You won't believe this," Joe said. "Look."

Sure enough, there she sat, skinny and dirty. She had unusual markings so there was no doubt it was she. She had walked eight miles of swamps, cornfields, wild animals, dogs, and gun-happy people who hate cats, and she'd crossed the dangerous road of trucks to get to us.

Joe and I looked at each other. In unison we said, "She stays." We opened the door, and the little stray walked in as if she'd always lived here.

"What about your allergy?" I asked.

"I'll take a decongestant," Joe said. "This cat walked back to us."

Used to the outdoors, the cat had some trouble with the first night indoors. But she was exhausted, and after wolfing down food, she fell sound asleep. We named her Kit Kat after the kitchen clock.

The next day, Joe dropped Kit Kat off at a vet's for shots and spaying, and the following day we went to pick her up. There was bad news.

"Your cat has a terminal illness," the vet said. "When we opened her up, we saw that she has feline infectious peritonitis (FIP) in the advanced stage. Lots of strays and feral cats get this. She is asymptomatic right now, but she isn't going to live a long life."

We were devastated. After much questioning, it turned out that Kit Kat probably didn't even have a year. "We can put her down if you'd like," the vet offered.

Before I had a chance to respond, Joe said firmly, "Absolutely not. This cat is a survivor, and she worked hard to get back to us. We'll take her home and keep her until she dies."

And so we took home our dying cat. That night, with stitches in her belly and a fresh pedicure, she caught a mouse. We were as pleased as could be.

Something else was going on in my life at the time. I was adopted at birth and had found the whereabouts of my biological mother many years ago. I wrote to her several times— even asked for medical history—but she never answered my letters. I could not know at the time that the night we took Kit Kat to the ranch, my mother died in a nearby town. I had never met her. Three days later, her friends tracked me down. They hadn't known she had a child at all until shortly before she died, and then only because they came across my letters. The letters were kept together in a place near her reading chair. For some reason, she could never bring herself to respond to me.

The day after we brought Kit Kat home from the vet, I went to my mother's memorial service. I learned that she had a wonderful laugh, that her confirmation verse had been "Make a joyful noise unto the Lord." I learned that her favorite song was "Mack the Knife," a detail I personally found particularly delightful for some reason. And that, like me, she was a voracious reader. I got to know her friends and my relatives. I was so happy that I had at least this much. Probably only adopted people can really understand this, but at the age of forty-six, for the first time in my life I felt grounded.

But I couldn't grieve. I felt distanced. After all, I did not know this woman. She gave birth to me, but I never knew her. I felt oddly detached among the mourners. I only wished she would have consented to see me before dying.

Back home, however, I suddenly found all kinds of maternal feelings rising in me toward Kit Kat. I have no children and had never felt these feelings before. But I found myself rocking Kit Kat and crying. Why was I crying? On the surface, I didn't want my little cat to die. But I really knew that she was the vehicle to help me connect to my deeply buried grief about the woman who bore me but would not know me.

Kit Kat would tolerate this for awhile, then she would jump down and go about her cat day. And I'd feel better. But I always prayed that I'd be able to handle it when she got sick.

Months went by. She didn't get sick. She got fat and sleek and turned into a gorgeous tortoiseshell. She was smart and quick, and she lived for Joe, who would get right down on the floor and play with her. She still liked us to watch her while she ate. Sometimes, if we left her alone for the day, she wouldn't eat until we came back and sat with her at her cat dish.

Joe took drugs for his allergies, and we agreed to keep Kit Kat out of the bedroom, thereby keeping one room dander-free. But Joe's allergy simply disappeared. Now both my cat and my husband were healthier than they were suppose to be!

After a few months, I took Kit Kat in to get her claws trimmed. It was the same clinic but a different vet. "How do you think her FIP is?" I asked.

The vet looked at me, then back at Kit Kat. "This cat has FIP?" she asked. "Who told you that?"

I paused. "This clinic told me."

The vet looked a little uncomfortable. "Did they see it in wet stages when they operated on her?"

"Yes," I said. "Doesn't she have it?"

"Well," she drawled, "sometimes other things look like FIP. The fact that your cat not only did not get sick but in fact got healthier makes me wonder. I'm not saying she has it, but I'm not saying she doesn't, either."

There is no test for FIP, so I took Kit Kat home, hardly daring to believe she might not die so soon.

Right around that time, I had a dream. It had been six months since my mother died, and in the dream, I was told that I could visit her. I went up in a jet. She entered it mid-flight from the back of the plane and came down the aisle, beaming at me. She sat next to me and curled around me, never speaking, just smiling. I told her all about myself, about my childhood and about my love of books. She nodded and almost cooed, but she never spoke.

I felt love radiate from her, and I felt something strongly maternal flow from her. I almost expected her to count my fingers and toes! I had the realization that in the next life, we get to be the individual God created each of us to be, before our walls go up and cloak parts of our personhood.

Eventually I knew she had to leave. She quietly held my hand. Then she got up, walked back down the aisle, and disappeared.

When I woke up, I felt almost as though I had had a visitation. I felt that I knew her suddenly, and I felt so very sorry that she could not bring down her own walls enough to know me in this life. For the first time, I felt grief. I cried for days.

Kit Kat took to climbing on me and kneading her paws into me as if she were nursing. She treated me as if I was her mother. I felt terribly protective. I felt her little claws and loved her and cried. I didn't think I could stand to lose her. I took her to a different vet.

"This cat does not have FIP," the vet proclaimed. "If she did, she'd be dead by now, and she certainly wouldn't be this hale and hearty." I consulted a third vet who said the same.

"Do you mean I may have her for many years?" I asked this one.

"No reason why not."

Did Kit Kat ever have FIP? Probably not, though I have friends who believe love healed her. My maternalism slowly relaxed, and my grief about my mother turned into the dull ache it needs to be. Joe and I both adore Kit Kat, though she's partial to him; when he's in the room, I cease to exist. But that's okay. He's her rescuer, her fellow cat. I'm her mother object. We are thankful every day that she survived and walked back to us.

I learned from Kit Kat. Abandoned, she nevertheless chose the way she would live. I was abandoned, too, and I have worked through those issues and have gotten on with life with a fresh appreciation for my adopted family.

We live in a fallen world. Kittens are thrown into the wild by cruel people. Mothers can't always keep their babies. But there are also small miracles: Kit Kat finding us, my people finding me, Kit Kat insisting that she is ours, Joe losing his allergy, my meeting my mother in a vivid dream, Kit Kat's clean bill of health. These are the things for which I am grateful. These are the ways I know my Creator watches over us.

I'm Right Here

*"Your friend is your needs answered.
He is your field which you sow with love
and reap with thanksgiving."*

KAHLIL GIBRAN

Loneliness is one of life's most difficult problems. Typically we're advised to get out and be with people, but sometimes being with other people can make us feel even more isolated.

Being with an animal, even one we don't know very well, is different. We don't feel as if we have to do anything to be accepted. It's like sitting on a park bench and feeding the birds. We're not lonely anymore. We're among friends, and all we have to do is be there for each other.

Yes, I Have Known Love

DIANE M. CIARLONI

My 27-year-old niece sat on the ottoman in front of my chair, facing me, her chin supported by her right hand. Her dark, almost-black eyes were still. They usually danced merrily, but not now. She was focused somewhere other than the here and now.

Beth and I share a much tighter bond than most aunt/niece relationships. Neither of us knows why. We just do. She looks like me and thinks like me. She feels like me and wishes like me. Her dreams belong to me and vice versa. There are times when it's almost—but not quite—frightening.

It was only the first of May and this was already her third visit of the year. That was unusual but there were circumstances. The first trip came when she was plunged into the middle of a painful divorce. The second was the week before a judge ruled a final decree and this one, the third, heralded the beginning of the rebuilding of her life.

She brought herself back to the present. I could almost see the hand-over-hand pull she used to cross the bridge linking wherever she'd been with now.

"Do you think you've ever really and truly known love?" she queried. "I mean . . . as in real love."

I hadn't anticipated the question but, given the prevailing circumstances, it didn't come as a shock.

"Yes," I said without hesitating. "I don't think . . . I know. I've known love."

Beth sat up straighter on the ottoman. A look of interest passed across her eyes. She was finally shifting the focus from herself to something—or someone—else.

"Who?" she asked.

"Why, there have been several," I responded.

"How many?"

I shrugged my shoulders. "At least ten. Maybe even more."

"Oh, come on," she said with a grin. "I know most of the family considers you . . . well . . . let's say they think you're rather unconventional. But TEN or more?! That's getting hard for even me to handle."

I leaned forward and planted a light kiss on her forehead. "That's because you're thinking in terms of people," I said, "or, more specifically, men."

She drew back with a question mark in her eyes. "Well? Aren't you?"

"Most certainly not," I said with a laugh. "I'm referring to Smudge, Duke, Spumone, Bob, Bubba, Doso, Kansas, Justine, Jellybean, Jingle, Jonah, Skipper. Count them! That's twelve, and I could go on!" Now she was laughing. "But those are animals," she chortled.

My tone turned serious. "And can you imagine a more perfect love than that?" I asked. "There are a lot of interesting points here if you look at them," I added. She waited.

"Think about it," I continued. "We read about *agape* love. . . . "

"God's perfect, unconditional love for us," she interrupted.

"Yes. Have you ever seen it in action other than in animals? There are people out there who're so quick to say we were given dominion over animals. I think they translate dominion as power and control rather than stewardship and caretaking. Besides, I once read in Job that God holds the soul of every living creature in His hand. Far be it from me to mistreat anything or anyone who enjoys a seat in God's palm."

Oprah, my black Cocker Spaniel, jumps on my chair and drapes herself across my lap. Without thinking, my hand reaches out and begins stroking her long ears. Beth catches the motion.

"But if God thinks animals are so important, why doesn't He let them live longer?"

I shrug my shoulders. "Lessons, I guess. We know, when we begin a relationship with an animal, that it'll last only a short time. We're lucky if we have them 12 to 15 years. What's that? Less than one-fifth of our lives? So we learn to value the time we have with them. We try to walk in love with them. We seldom yell at them and, if we do, we hurriedly apologize or hug them or hand them an extra doggie or kitty treat. We feel badly if we do anything to mar that brief time we've been granted with them. We treasure each 24 hours and, when we see the first gray hairs in their muzzles, we look the other way because we can't bear to think about that inevitable day. And we never say, 'I'll hug them tomorrow or tell them I love them later.' Are we like that with our spouses? Or with our children or our parents? Or friends? No. We never look at those relationships as fragile and short-lived.

"I think we seldom learn the lesson, but I think God uses animals to teach us how to love more openly, to love for each day, to value each hour, and to regret anything we may do to soil or spoil that love."

Oprah pushes against me. She doesn't have enough room on the chair so I move over to accommodate her. It makes me a bit uncomfortable but—so what?

"Have you ever noticed how people talk about dead people?" Beth asked.

"What do you mean?"

"Well, let's say someone's husband or wife dies. Suddenly, the person who died is a saint! He or she never did or said anything wrong. Or, at least, that's the way it sounds if you listen to the one who's still alive."

"You're right," I said with a smile, "but I don't know why it happens like that." I reach over and begin stroking Oprah with both hands. "Maybe it's for the same reason we find it so difficult to write about our animals while they're still alive."

Beth looks at me. "Remember how we taught Oprah to suck pieces of hard candy from our mouths when she was a baby?"

"Oh, I remember," I thought to myself, "but remembering things that happened nearly 12 years ago makes me think I'm using up my bank account with the beloved Cocker. If I'm already drawing on memories, does it mean there are very few future deposits remaining?"

No papers accompanied Oprah. She cost $50 at the local feed store, and there was the faintest hint of something other than Cocker Spaniel in her gene pool. Whatever it was remained well hidden because, as far as the world was concerned, Oprah was an absolutely beautiful Cocker. People stopped me in the vet's office or on the sidewalk or wherever to comment on her coat. It resembled black patent leather with a hand-rubbed shine. Her baby head was a delicately rounded dome balanced by long, curly, miniature ears on either side. Her snoot was the lovely American, rather than English, version of the breed.

Oprah was smart, and house-training went smoothly. She wanted to please and, of course, she did. And, I simply altered the level of my expectations on the rare times she fell short, which meant everyone ended up happy.

I remember her first Christmas. A huge tree was positioned in the living room and ornaments were spread from one wall to the other. She was still a pup, and had been gently scolded several times about running roughshod through all the breakables. Suddenly, I became aware that I hadn't heard from her in several minutes. I turned to look and there, sitting a few feet away, was a statue-still Cocker puppy gently holding an ornament. It dangled from her white teeth by a red ribbon. That, of course, merited a very long hug.

I'd never had a Cocker so I didn't know how they were supposed to look as babies. I remember being out one day and seeing a lady with a blonde Cocker on a leash. It was an adult, all done up in the traditional Cocker "do." I wailed and moaned, quite certain my slick-coated pup would never have enough hair for a beauty parlor outing. I was wrong. It wasn't long before she made the trip every three weeks. She hated her first grooming just as much as she hated her most recent one. Some things just don't change.

Yes, Beth remembered correctly. We did allow Oprah to suck hard candy from our mouths. Oh, I know, it sounds really gross but it was also hysterically funny. Some people say she's a beggar when she does things such as rest her chin on my knee when I'm eating, rolling her eyes until only the whites are visible. I, on the other hand, prefer to say she's concentrating rather than begging. Anyway, she knew Beth and I had something edible in our mouths and, to tease her, we leaned forward and allowed her to press the end of her mouth against our lips. Then we parted our lips just slightly and . . . suck! She had the candy! And she enjoyed the candy! John, my husband, chastised our behavior mightily but we ignored him.

Oprah grew. Her hair lengthened and her ears assumed luxurious proportions. Her body muscled and hardened while her eyes retained their loving softness. And, over the years, those heart-frightening gray hairs began creeping into her muzzle. She and I seemed to breathe as one. She knew what I was going to do as soon as my hand or leg or head moved. She posed for photographs in front of flowers and trees and, once, in the middle of a field of Texas bluebonnets and Indian paintbrush. John took a picture of the two of us together in that same field and it's since been used on book covers. Framed and matted, her image stares at us from numerous spots on our walls.

Perhaps it's my imagination but Oprah seemed to develop a posture as she matured. Her love was always there, but her puppy emotions changed into something that said "I love you so much. Just let me sit next to you and be with you in your chair or stretch out next to you in bed. But even if you put me outside, I'll still love you. You just can't make me change. I'll do anything for you and, if you choose, you needn't do anything for me."

She's, well, she's solid. She's there. It doesn't matter how turbulent my life might become or how many storms rage around me. She never moves. She never wavers. Some people say the unmoving earth beneath their feet provides their stability. Not me. I've lived in California and I've been rocked by earthquakes. For me, Oprah is my stability.

Things are changing. It seems each day brings more gray hair. In her muzzle, yes; but now they also fleck across her back and sides. They look silver against the midnight black. She's developed a disc problem in her back. It seems to flare up more and more frequently with deeper and deeper severity. It causes her tremendous pain, and she can find no comfortable position. I try to help her but there's nothing I can do. She cries when I lift her to put her in the car for a trip to the vet, and my heart breaks. He places her on medications for two weeks, with the list including Prednisone. The latter is a derivative of cortisone, and extended use isn't good. One of its side effects, with her, is that she's unable to hold her urine. She may urinate while sleeping, or while awake, and never know it until she realizes she's wet. Then she smells herself or the carpet or the furniture and realizes what happened. She's confused, wondering how she could have done such a thing. She feels bad, knowing such behavior is unacceptable. With my heart literally hurting, I hasten to reassure her. I tell her soiled carpet or furniture is a very, very small price to pay for having her. I put a rubber sheet on my side of the bed during our last bout with Prednisone. Some people would call me crazy. Maybe, but I say that's part of being so confident that I really and truly have known love—just as Beth asked.

I have no way of knowing how many more gray hairs will grace Oprah's muzzle before she leaves me. She still bucks and jumps and races around the house like a puppy when her back is quiet. Her eyes dance when I ask "Who wants to go potty?" She leads the way, and tells everyone else when they may or may not pass through the door. In other words, she rules the roost and enjoys every moment of her reign. She knows how to get her way with me. It doesn't require a great deal. Just a look or two. She's a fountainhead of love and forgiveness and encouragement. None of that ever changes. Like God, she's the same today as she was yesterday, and she'll still be the same tomorrow. That's why she's Oprah. She loves me blindly, and I have no doubt she'd lay down her life for me. And, as for me, I never put off until tomorrow telling her I love her in return.

So go ahead, as Beth did, and ask me. Say to me, "Have you ever really and truly loved and been loved?"

I'll say to you, "Yes, of course. I have loved and been loved, really and truly, by Spumone and Justine and Smudge and Kansas and Doso and Bubba and Jingle and Jellybean and Jonah and Highway, and ever, ever so much by Oprah and. . . . They are my litany of love, my rosary of compassion and my mantra of caring concern.

"Ah, yes. I am blessed. I am loved."

Just an Ordinary Cat

LORRIE KREIGSCH

We had no intention of ever getting a cat. We had raised hamsters (a mother and 7 babies) and a rabbit (which was won at a carnival) but that was it as far as animals went.

Until one day . . . we were visiting a friend in Pittsburgh, PA and were told we just had to see this new little cat that had wandered into her life. She was a beautiful pure black cat with not a speck of white on her. Her fur was so soft, like velvet. This cat came over to me under the picnic table and wanted some petting. Then she let me pick her up and started licking me with her sandpaper-like tongue. I fell in love with her right away. The friend asked if we would like to take her home with us (as she already had a Husky) but we declined.

Once I got home, I began to miss that little critter and told my husband I wanted her. He called the friend and the offer was still open. So two weeks later we again made the two-hour trip to Pittsburgh just to pick up the cat. She was so well behaved that she sat on my lap the whole way home without even moving.

We called her Ebony for obvious reasons and she only had one little flaw—one of her eyes seemed to be injured and wouldn't slit. The veterinarian said she probably ran into something, but I feel she may have been abused because she hid under the bed when any kids came to the house and she dreaded the broom and vacuum cleaner. All I had to do was bring out the broom from the closet and she was gone.

But Ebony soon came to trust us and she turned out to be a fantastic companion. She would sleep on the bed, draping herself around my head, just like a pillow. She would give little kisses with her tongue, which felt less and less like sandpaper. In the morning, she would lick me all over just as if she were washing another cat. When I didn't feel well, she would just lie by my side, purring away and giving little kisses until I felt better and got up.

We had many conversations and she would always let me know, with her deep, husky voice, when things were not going exactly her way. Off she would go, pouting, to the other room.

She was my shadow, following me wherever I went, and always was there to greet me when I came home. She helped me with all my household chores, such as pouncing on the sheets to help get out the wrinkles, walking on the clean floors to see if they were dry, helping me put the groceries away by making sure I didn't forget anything in the bags, helping me fold the laundry by going into my clothes basket, and helping me wrap Christmas presents by walking all over the paper.

When I would sit down with a book or some craft, she would waste no time in jumping on my lap and making sure I paid some attention to her, too.

We didn't let her loose outside since we live beside a major highway and just recently had seen a neighbor cat get killed by a car, but we did let her out on the porch with us when we went out. Most of the time she behaved, but once in awhile, she got a little mischievous streak in her. She would climb down the stairs, look back to see if we were watching, go a little farther in the yard, look back and see if we were still watching and make a game of it to see how far she could go before I called her back.

One time Ebony was outside when a neighbor dog came bounding into the yard after her and she just huddled behind me for protection and I was ready to tackle that dog for her. I took care of her and she took care of me.

But one day I couldn't take care of her anymore. She stopped eating and wouldn't come out of her little corner, which was just not like her. We took her to the veterinarian for tests and when the news came back, it was not good. Ebony was in the final stages of kidney failure, which is fatal. But how could this be? We only had her for nine short years and it happened so quickly. We were told that there really are no symptoms for kidney failure until it is too late, and it is a very common disease in cats. While that didn't really help the situation at all, it did give us peace of mind that there was nothing we could have done to prevent it.

So we said goodbye to Ebony but it was the darkest day of my life. All the light and life had gone out of me. She was not just a cat, she was my baby, and I just wanted to die with her. For a long time, I saw her everywhere I looked—that's the spot in which she sunned herself, that's the place where she used to sleep, that's the window where she sat to watch the birds, that's the corner where she ate her food. Even now, four years later, tears still come to my eyes when I see a black cat or something happens to trigger a fond memory of her.

Eventually Tess, a calico cat, and Miko, a gray tiger-striped cat, came into our lives to fill the void left by Ebony. While they are special in their own way, they will never replace Ebony.

They are not lappers and not lickers and that special bond between us is still missing, but we are working on it.

Ebony taught me many things. She taught me persistence: to never give up until I get what I want. She taught me patience: some things are just longer in coming than others. She taught me the art of observance: to enjoy and appreciate nature. She taught me to be there for people and listen: sometimes that's all it takes to comfort someone. Most of all, she taught me what it felt like to love and be loved in return. Eb, I sure do miss you!

Ebony was just an ordinary cat with a flaw, but she was perfect and special in my eyes. That's how it is with God, too. We are just ordinary people with flaws, but we are special in His eyes. Sometimes the bond is there and sometimes we have to work on it, but He will always be there for us with an unconditional love.

Another Day
Was Born

NANCY B. GIBBS

From the time I was a small child, I always loved the ocean. My mind can easily get lost while gazing across the sea, even though a busy world may surround me. My favorite time at the beach is the moment when the sun peeks over the horizon. My dream vacation would be to spend days, weeks or even months on the shoreline, watching each day as it is born.

During one spring break, our family gathered up our belongings and went to spend an entire week at Jekyll Island, Georgia. In my opinion, that island is paradise on earth, a true gift from God. My toy poodle, Daisey, loves vacations, too! I don't go anywhere without her. Thank God for motels that allow pets in the guest rooms.

My plans were to be on the beach each morning to welcome the sun. My family's plans were quite different from mine. For some odd reason, they wanted to sleep away their vacation. "That's okay," I thought. "Daisey will go along with me."

Knowing that the early morning air would be brisk, I took Daisey's little red sweater with us. The first morning, I arose before the sun. I got dressed and put Daisey's sweater on her, and together we went to welcome the day.

The wind was blowing and Daisey's long ears danced in the breeze. We walked along the coastline, enjoying every single second of the early-morning spectacular. "Look at the sun, Daisey!" I shouted, as I picked her up and we watched the ball of fire rise above the water. She cuddled up close to me.

The next morning, Daisey and I got up early and went to greet the sun. I gathered seashells and enjoyed the solitude that we shared on the beach. Then we had a busy day filled with bike riding and a historical tour of the island.

When I went to bed that night, I decided that I would sleep late the next morning. Just before the sun rose, however, I heard an insistent scratching on the door. I reached over to the side of the bed and flipped on the lamp. Daisey was standing at the door and scratching on it while holding her little red sweater in her mouth.

I laughed and jumped up out of bed. I quickly got dressed and then put Daisey's sweater on her. Off we went to greet the sun, as another day was born.

I discovered one thing for certain that morning. People are not the only creatures who love the ocean. Poodles do, too!

Disney: Love of My Life

TONI EAMES

He was my passion and soul mate, but none of my friends shared my adoration. Disney was a cat so bonded to me, he regarded the rest of the world as intrusive enemies.

When I first met that four-week-old orphaned kitty at the League for Animal Protection in Long Island, New York, he won my heart immediately by climbing up my back and nestling in the crook of my neck. With high hopes for a frolicking, fun-loving and entertaining new housemate, I named him Disney to commemorate my recent visit to Disneyland. Placing the 12-ounce gray tabby in a cardboard carrying case, I set off for home and our new life together.

Determining from the start that there would be no barrier between us, Disney crawled out of the box and into my coat pocket! This need for physical closeness remained a pattern we shared throughout our life together.

On arriving at my apartment in Jamaica, Queens, I set about bottle-feeding the little guy. However, Disney indicated that he was ready to be a big boy and weaned himself on the spot. Exploring my tiny apartment, he found and used the litter box and settled for the night in bed with me and Flicka, my Golden Retriever guide dog.

Wanting my adorable kitten to be well socialized, I brought

him to work with me at least twice a week. After resting quietly in the carrier as I walked to the Long Island Rail Road, Disney curled on my shoulder during the hour-long train ride to Long Island. In my office at Kings Park Psychiatric Center, he was pampered by co-workers and patients. Despite every effort to shape him into a loving, caring and outgoing cat, by the time he reached puberty, and despite the fact of having been neutered, he wanted no part of anyone who wasn't me! The one lasting benefit of these early excursions was that he became a restful and quiet traveler.

Disney poured his passion into his relationship with Flicka and me. Having worn out his welcome on the job by growling and hissing at patients and fellow workers, Disney, who now had to be left home, greeted me each evening by flinging himself into my arms, putting his paws around my neck and licking my face. Totally tuned into my every mood, he followed me around the house taking advantage of every opportunity to sit in my lap or maintain physical contact. When I cried, he tried to lick the tears away. When my beloved Flicka was diagnosed with terminal cancer, Disney's opportunity to minister to my unhappiness reached its zenith.

After Golden Retriever Ivy came to live with us during her training as Flicka's successor, Disney was ecstatic with his new canine buddy. Ivy learned that Disney enjoyed being nuzzled and flipped in the air, and this soon became their favorite game!

One of my weekend relaxations was lying in bed, talking on the phone, while Disney and Ivy sprawled on either side of me. When blind friends visited my apartment, Disney warmly welcomed their guide dogs, but made it apparent that the human guests were a considerable annoyance. My friend Bob commented that Disney's hisses were like the hum of the refrigerator—just so much background noise! Others quipped that they maintained our friendship despite Disney. These negative, but well-deserved comments, caused me to become even more bonded to and protective of my one-woman feline.

After Flicka's death, Ivy, mentored by Flicka, smoothly took over the essential role of guide. Wanting to provide companionship for Disney during the long days I was away at work, I adopted another cat. Despite his growing antipathy toward humans, Disney quickly adjusted to the addition of Tevye, our new feline family member. However, his adjustment to my new husband, Ed, was less than tranquil. Always ready to make friends with members of the animal kingdom, Disney immediately welcomed Ed's black Labrador guide dog, Perrier, but resented Ed's intrusion into our lives.

Somehow, sensing this intruder was permanent, Disney did not display his usual hostility by hissing and spitting. However, he did not allow Ed to touch him and never voluntarily climbed into his lap. A stealthy hunter, Disney would take advantage of Ed's blindness and unfamiliarity with cunning feline tactics like swooping onto the table and swiping any unguarded food on Ed's plate. In contrast, I was never a target of his marauding ways.

On one memorable evening, Ed prepared to heat a large chunk of leftover steak. Placing the meat in a frying pan, Ed momentarily turned away from the stove. Not one to pass up such a splendid opportunity, Disney snatched the cold meat and took cover under the bed with his booty. Ed raised such a ruckus, I ran into the kitchen, assuming some dire emergency had occurred. As Ed continued ranting and raving, I reached under the bed, grabbed a snarling Disney by the scruff of his neck and ripped the chunk of meat away from him!

Sharpening his hunting skills by successfully stalking and snatching food from Ed's plate, led Disney into a new career— stalking and capturing mice. Our apartment building went through a period of mice invasions. Disney, a totally indoor cat, let his instincts take over whenever one of those unfortunate rodents entered our home. In typical cat fashion, he dropped these gifts on my pillow and in my shoe. Lucky Ed, whom Disney did not deem worthy of being showered by loving offerings, did not have to unexpectedly encounter the victims of Disney's prowess!

When we decided to settle in California, Disney, a seasoned traveler, lay quietly in his carrier under the seat during the cross-country flight. With a large California town house to explore, Disney was in his element. Sitting on the kitchen windowsill, he was able to monitor the comings and goings of our neighbors. As long as they stayed outside, he was content to be the passive observer. Should any friend or neighbor enter the house, however, Disney reverted to his guarding mode, greeting them with hisses and growls. We joked that if anyone broke into our house, it would be Disney, not the dogs, who would scare the intruder away.

Whenever I left the house, Disney took up guard-cat duty on the windowsill. As soon as I turned the corner and approached the house or got out of a car, he would impatiently start meowing on catching sight of me. As I entered the house, he would launch himself from the nearby kitchen counter into my arms. With the key still in the door, I would have to drop Ivy's leash to brace for my flying feline!

As our Fresno friendship network expanded, Disney's reputation became legendary. When people entered our home, the dogs gleefully greeted them, Tevye explored their bags and belongings, and Disney disdainfully glared at them. He would position himself midway up the stairs and dare anyone to intrude on his territory. It was the rare individual willing to challenge this 10-pound enforcer by going upstairs. Based on their experience, friends were quick to believe my story that the tiger cub I held in a picture hanging on the upstairs wall was Disney's mother!

Since Disney was not hostile to new dogs, he became useful in the training of assistance-dog puppies. Fresno-based puppies being socialized to become future guide, service and hearing dogs, were brought to the house to learn proper cat etiquette from our miniature tiger. Disney taught them that sniffs and occasional licks were permissible, but nipping, chasing and frenetic activity were not. As with humans, feline smacks, hisses and snarls could control the most exuberant canine behavior. When these puppies later assumed their careers as assistance dogs, their new partners marveled at the acquired cat etiquette they displayed.

At the age of 12, Disney began displaying signs of failing health. For several weeks, he had bouts of diarrhea and vomiting. Completely traumatized by what might lie ahead, we made the 150-mile trip to a specialty veterinary practice. Dr. Helen Hamilton made the diagnosis of intestinal cancer and said Disney would have to be hospitalized for a week following surgery. I could not imagine how my wild cat would cope in a strange environment completely cut off from me. Realizing we would both suffer separation anxiety, I cuddled my striped boy and tearfully left him with Dr. Hamilton.

Disney, labeled as a classic case of Feline Hysterical Syndrome by the veterinarians who had treated him in the past, was far from an ideal patient. His week-long stay turned out to be not only traumatic for Disney and me, but also for the hospital staff. Inconsolable at home, I phoned first thing in the morning and last thing at night for progress reports. Dr. Hamilton phoned daily to update Ed and me on Disney's physical status. He was progressing medically, but was virtually impossible for the staff to handle without sedation. Toward the end of his hospital stay, I asked Dr. Hamilton if Disney was one of the worst patients she ever had. After a short pause, she said, "No, he isn't one of the worst; he is the worst!"

With great anticipation at the reunion with my soul mate, we again made the three-hour trip to the specialty hospital. Intimidated by this ferocious patient, the staff debated how best to wrestle him from the hospital cage into his carrying case. I assured them Disney would not hurt me and would calmly allow me to lift him out of the cage. The hospital staff were astonished when I picked up a raging Disney and he was immediately transformed into a clinging, loving kitty. Upon hearing my voice, he flung himself into my arms, put his front paws around my neck and covered my face with kisses. The entire staff came running to witness this miraculous transformation!

Thinking the crisis was over, we were emotionally unprepared for the ensuing ordeal. Several days after returning home, Disney developed a severe upper respiratory tract infection which quickly spread to the other cats. They stopped eating, required syringe feeding, subcutaneous fluids and lots of medication.

Whenever we have faced crises, guardian angels have appeared on the scene. This time our guardian angel came in the form of Michelle Lopez, a veterinary technician familiar with our furry family. Michelle took time out of her busy schedule to come to our home twice a day to minister to our ailing felines.

In his weakened state, Disney allowed Michelle to handle him, and as days stretched into weeks, regained his strength but not his fierceness. Our bond became even greater. He rarely left my side, and slept in the crook of my arms at night with his paw touching my face. In the morning, he followed me into the bathroom and sat on the sink while I prepared for the day. He developed the habit of standing on my foot until I reached down to scoop him into my arms.

From the beginning, Dr. Hamilton indicated the surgery was not a cure for the intestinal cancer. Without Michelle I would not have had the extra year with my passion kitty. I cherished each day, and when his health again began to fail, I faced one of the most difficult decisions of my life. When I lost my guide dogs to death, I knew another Golden Retriever would have a similar temperament and could assume the guiding role. I anguished that once my beloved cat and I were parted, there would never be another Disney. After his death, friends, although personally glad he was gone, lovingly extended a hand to me in my inconsolable grief.

My memory of a very special time in my life with a very special friend is deeply embedded in my heart. Disney's outrageous behavior has reached mythical proportions as our friends tell and re-tell the nature of their encounters with him.

Although I now share my life with four wonderful kitties and no one is afraid to visit, I still deeply miss my soul mate.

A Hero for All Seasons

CAROL FLEISCHMAN

*B*eing a blind woman, I depended on my guide dog, Misty, for mobility. When she died, however, the help she gave me was overshadowed by the void left from a nine-year partnership filled with love and mutual care.

Whenever Misty heard the buckle jingle as I pulled the harness from its hook, my partner dashed to my side, eager to work. People told me that when I spoke to her, she rotated her black velvety ears as she decoded my words. When out of harness, she frequently stole napkins from our dinner guests and caught tennis balls with ease. Most of all, though, Misty worked tirelessly so I could be independent. That meant she stopped at curbs and waited for my next command. When we successfully reached the opposite curb, I'd visualize her erect ears hearing the words, "Good girl!"

In spring, Misty would take me around low-hanging branches that dripped with their fragrant blooms. In summer, she would take me around a forgotten bike lying across the sidewalk. In autumn, we would walk through the leaves crunching beneath our feet, and she would not be startled by the ferocious hum of street-sweeping equipment. In winter, we moved with the grace of ice skaters on neighborhood sidewalks.

Throughout the year, we shared work and play. Misty dozed

under my computer desk and we posed for pictures on a beach blanket. One weekend, my husband, Misty, and I stayed in a bed and breakfast which had been owned by a rice planta-tion owner in North Carolina. During his ownership, the dismal lower level was used to house slaves. Two hundred years later, due to the Americans with Disabilities Act, Misty enjoyed stretching out before the fireplace in the spacious, beautifully decorated room.

Maybe Misty's paw print, like an ink stain, is indelible on my heart because she was a miracle worker. She erased my fear of dogs—I had never even owned a pet.

Before getting her, a simple stroll in the neighborhood could put me in a panic; muscles tightened and my pulse raced. My ears strained, listening for the jingle of collar tags coming closer as dogs made a bee-line for me.

"Oh, don't worry. Buddy won't bite." These words from the owner were not comforting. However, neither was the thought of being tethered to my house. Freedom had a strong pull on me and that motivation pointed the way to the Seeing Eye for my first guide dog.

As my "leading lady," none of Misty's beauty went un-noticed. All of her sixty pounds were wrapped in a sleek, black coat that caught the attention of everyone, especially puzzled children: "Mom, is that a dog or a wolf?"

When I became a reformed animal lover, many doors opened, since my furry "ice breaker" allowed me to meet other dog enthusiasts. Some of them got so excited seeing a guide dog working that they mixed up their adjectives: "Oh, there's one of those blind dogs!"

I lived with a hero who didn't get a six-figure salary, but she got plenty of praise and affection. Misty never rode in a limousine, but I learned that a commercial airline pilot saluted her as we stepped off a plane. The White House never sent a telegram honoring her, but I received bundles of sympathy cards and tributes in her memory.

Now, a new guide dog must come into my home and not step on the paws of a beloved ghost. There's room in my heart for a successor, but I feel that Misty will always be guiding both of us.

Fine Feathered Friends

GINA ROMSDAHL

"Quack! Quaaaack!" I believe the translation from duck language into human terms would be interpreted as "Can Gina come out to play?" Every morning, the duck would come to the back door and call for me to come out and join him, which I happily did. It was our morning ritual.

I was only 2 or 3 years old. The duck had belonged to the former tenant's son, and when the family moved they left the duck behind. My family adopted the duck, and the duck adopted me. Using all the worldly references my young mind possessed, I named the duck "Donald." Donald's feathers were white and his feet and bill were a muted orange. He looked like his namesake, minus the little blue sailor suit, of course.

Donald followed me everywhere I went. He would grasp my sundress or shorts in his bill and we would chug along like a whimsical choo-choo train. I was the engine and Donald was the caboose.

It was very hot in Fresno, California, and we had a plastic wading pool in the backyard. It was a small pool, by adult standards, but it was plenty big enough for Donald and me. We spent hours cooling off in the pool, splashing and playing together. Who needs a rubber ducky, when you have the real thing?

Although our backyard was relatively small and fenced in, my mother panicked one afternoon because she couldn't find me anywhere. There was no sign of me or of Donald, and she knew we had to be together, but where? The yard was empty and the pool lay still and motionless. My mother frantically called my Uncle Abe and pleaded for help. Abe rushed to her aid, and they began a thorough search of the neighborhood. Eventually I was found, fast asleep in my own backyard. In order to escape the heat of the day, I had crawled under a bush and fallen asleep. Donald was at my side, watching over me. Donald was my guardian angel, and he even had the wings to prove it. He was my best friend and I loved him with all my heart.

It all came to an end one afternoon when my mother and I returned home from a short errand. I gaily ran into the backyard to tell my fine feathered friend that I was home. I was shocked by a sight that I shall never, ever forget. In our short absence, someone had stolen into our yard and slit my friend's throat. It had to have just happened, because Donald was still alive, barely. Perhaps our arrival home had interrupted the murderer in progress. Donald's head was separated from his body by a few inches, but there was a long string of some kind, perhaps his spinal cord, that was still attached to both ends. Donald's eyes were like magnets, locking onto mine, and I understood completely the last message he conveyed to me with his eyes. There was fear there, and confusion, of the sudden and unexpected attack on his life. And there was something else. There was a sorrow and an apology, as if he understood that he was leaving me alone and had somehow failed in his duty.

My mother whisked me away from the grisly scene as the

last light in Donald's eyes flickered out. But I had received Donald's final gift to me, one that has affected the course of my life ever since. I understood that communication is possible between members of different species; between a two-year-old girl who can barely speak English and a duck that, if it speaks any language at all, is beyond our reckoning. Communication is possible because all life forms are connected, one to another, by the common experience of life itself. Every being has a desire to live, and a right to do so by virtue of the very fact of its existence. Empathy is the gateway to communication and understanding.

We never found out who murdered Donald, or why. It wouldn't have brought Donald back, in any case. However, a new duck would soon enter my life, and even though no one could ever replace Donald, I still had room in my heart for a new friend.

My Uncle Abe told his fifth-grade class the story of his niece and her pet duck, including Donald's tragic demise. One of the students was so touched that he generously brought my uncle a duckling and asked him to give it to his niece. There came my Uncle Abe up our walkway, cardboard box and duckling in tow, to deliver the present. I was delighted and promptly named him Donald II.

Donald II also had white feathers, but was distinguishable from Donald I by the patch of black feathers at the top of his head. As he was still quite small, we kept him inside the house at night, making a cardboard nest for him. This Donald and I spent most of our days outside playing and swimming together, but we feared to leave him alone, lest he meet the same fate as the first Donald. We always made sure that he was never unattended outside, and he had to come inside when we did.

Donald II and I became good friends, and were literally inseparable, due to the concern for his safety. As he grew older and bigger, it became more and more impractical to keep him inside, as well as unfair to deprive him of his outdoor heritage. Finally my parents made the decision to take Donald II to the zoo and release him. There was a lake at the zoo, and a number of ducks and other birds made their home there. Donald would be able to live his life in freedom and in the company of others of his own kind. It was surely in Donald's best interests to do this, but my young mind didn't see it that way. All I knew was that I was being asked to give up my friend.

Marginally convinced that it was the right thing to do, I accompanied my parents to the zoo on the fateful day of relocating Donald to his new home. We took him to the edge of the lake, released him, and headed back to the car. Donald was in hot pursuit behind us, flapping and squawking his indignation at being left behind. We tried again. And again. Each time, Donald would hurry after me, confused and flustered and upset. I was tormented. My doubts were confirmed—he wanted to be with me and he should be with me. We were abandoning him in the face of his loyalty. I felt wretched and woefully undeserving of his devotion. I stayed in the car, tears streaming down my face, while my father escorted Donald one last time to the lake and rushed back to the car for our getaway. We left him there, and I was haunted by the image of our cruel desertion.

We went back to the zoo every weekend for several weeks to see how he was adjusting. At first, Donald welcomed our visits and came to greet us excitedly. On subsequent visits, he became more and more hesitant to approach us, although he clearly recognized us. Perhaps it was difficult for him to reconcile our visits with his new life, or perhaps the inevitable rejection of our departure necessitated the breaking away of the bonds that had held us together. On our final visit, we saw Donald contentedly swimming in the lake with the other ducks. He stood out amongst the others because of the black markings on his head. If he saw or recognized us, he gave no indication. It appeared that he may even have acquired a mate, for there was another duck swimming closely by his side. I could see that Donald had survived the transition, and even appeared to be thriving. My friend was happy, and that was all that mattered. The burden of guilt slid from my shoulders and I was finally at peace.

There is a saying that sometimes "You have to be cruel to be kind." It's a hard lesson to learn, but there is truth in it.

I have had many animal companions since childhood, but Donald was the first. I will never forget him and the doorway to compassion that he opened in my heart.

Sweet As Sugar

JAN ROGERS

*S*he came to me unexpectedly, and seeing her that first time was quite a shock. She belonged to one of the men who was remodeling my house, and he brought her to my place to graze on all my long and lush grass, which is exactly what she was doing when I pulled into the driveway and saw her for the first time.

The look of her legs made me gasp; how she could even walk on them was both a mystery and a miracle. Both of her legs were grotesquely bent outward above her knees, and inward below them. The knees themselves were twice the size that they should have been, and her hooves had not been trimmed for ages.

Her name was "Minnie" but they called her "Gramma" because she was old, twenty-five, I was told, but none of it was true. I later learned that she was actually thirty-five, and her real name was "Mindy." None of it mattered, of course. I loved the horse from the moment I saw her, and decided then and there that this was where she'd remain. It really didn't matter what her name was, as she was as close to being totally deaf as she was ever going to be, but because she was as sweet as sugar, that's what I started calling her. Sugar, who greeted me whenever she saw me with her low, mellow nicker. Sugar, who loved to be touched, brushed and talked to, despite years of cruel and thoughtless treatment. I cried after I heard her sad story from the shameless man who had year after year forced her to endure what must have been agony.

When she was still a young mare she had been in a trailer that had crumbled around her in a crash, crushing her front legs. One or both of her knees had been broken, but she was never seen by a vet. Instead, she was left to heal unaided, as best she could, which wasn't very well. But that wasn't all. As soon as she was able to bear her own weight, she was used year after year for breeding. The extra weight of each endless pregnancy must have been an excruciating pain to bear on her poor, broken and deformed legs. The man who was working for me was actually allowing his four kids, aged seven to fourteen, to ride her, when no weight at all should have been on her back. By the time she came to me, her back sagged piteously, and every step was a struggle. But struggle she did, getting up every morning without complaint, to chew the tasty green grass that continued to last long past the time when other pastures had turned to the ochre of an oncoming winter.

I found out only by chance that her current owner was planning to have her removed while I was at work (now that she was sufficiently fattened on grass and the sweet grain and treats that I bought for her). His plan was to sell her at auction, where he had to know that she would go to slaughter. I learned of it the day before it was to happen, and angrily called him at home. I told him that I would buy her from him.

When he showed up the next day for work, he found that what he had heard from me the night before was only a warm-up for what he heard from me then. I found that I couldn't stop myself from telling him exactly what I thought of him, and none of it was very warm or friendly. I told him that he would have to answer for what he had planned to do to this horse in his "life review," and that no God I knew would look kindly upon him.

I heard myself go on and on, and wondered where my brakes had gone, but I couldn't stop. I knew that I myself was being unkind and causing another to feel uncomfortable, but I was so outraged that I had to let it out. In retrospect, I realize that I was reacting to every cruelty that Sugar had endured, and giving all of my sorrow and anger to only one of those responsible for her troubles. But he was the one who was willing to put her through an incredible agony, all for a few dollars, while I was paying him better than anyone else had in years. I wasn't sorry for my stinging words, and only stopped them when it occurred to me that if I didn't, he might take a loss on her and send her to slaughter just to spite me.

In the end I bought her for fifty dollars, far less than I was prepared to pay for her. Her former owner lost his job the day that I acquired the sweetest horse I've ever known, and it was a trade-off that I've never regretted.

The first thing I did was have the vet and a horseshoer come out and work on Sugar's hooves, hoping that it would make her more comfortable, and allow her to get around more easily. It did, and she began following me around like a puppy. She even tried to follow me into the house a time or two, and if there had been room in there for her, I probably would have let her come in. I continued to concentrate on getting her in the best shape possible all through that winter, and we became the best of friends.

Spring came, and Sugar happily and hungrily greeted the new and tender shoots of grass. She was looking much healthier, and I knew she was, at last, a happy horse. I hoped I'd have her with me for many more springs, so much a part of my life had she become.

In the middle of April, I had a vivid and beautiful dream that I was watching Sugar run in a field of wildflowers, and her legs were perfect; she was young again. I awoke with a feeling of happiness that soon turned to dread, as I realized that the dream might mean that Sugar was dead, released from the shackles that were her own legs, and running once more, beyond this life.

I bounded out of bed and yanked some clothes on, and ran outside to find her. I was greeted by her gentle whinny, velvet-brown nose, and lovely soft eyes. I was so relieved that I cried with happiness, not knowing what was to come.

On May first, I didn't see her in the morning. "She must be sleeping in," I thought. When I still hadn't seen her after an hour or so, I went looking for her, expecting the worst. I couldn't find her at first, and expanded my search, really worried by then. I found her in the sumac, still alive, but in bad shape. She called to me when she saw me, just as she always did, and I burst into tears.

She must have stumbled in the thick sumac; why she would have been grazing there, I don't know, but when she fell, she fell with her legs heading uphill, making it impossible for her to get up. I raced back up to the house and called a neighbor for help, then hurried down to where she lay, helpless, bringing her food and water. She was thirsty and hungry, and I realized then that she might have fallen as long ago as the evening before. I waited with her, frantic inside, for my neighbor to get there. My hope was that together we could flip her over and get her into a position that would allow her to get up.

I prayed that she would be able to get up, and that she would be all right.

When my neighbor arrived, we struggled to turn her to her other side, only to find, when we were finally successful, that a slender sumac trunk had pierced her side when she went down. How serious her injury was we couldn't tell, but I ran back up to the house to call for the vet to come out.

The vet couldn't come; his wife had just had a premature baby, but he told me to come and get some injections that might help Sugar. I hung up the phone and returned to the pasture to find my neighbor jubilant—Sugar was standing up and drinking from a five-gallon bucket. Just as I was about to shout my delight and thanks to him, I witnessed my sweet horse suddenly collapse and crash to the ground in a heap, hitting her head hard on the ground in the process. I screamed out her name as I ran to where she lay, and when I reached her, she greeted me with her soft whinny. I was sobbing uncontrollably by then, but I tried to comfort her, telling her that she'd be okay, she just needed to rest, that I'd come back with some medicine to make her stronger.

I sped to the vet's office, crying all the way. A part of me knew what the outcome was going to be, but as long as she was alive and wanted to try to get up, I felt that I had to do whatever I could to help her. The vet gave me the injections and promised to come to my farm for her the following day if need be.

I returned home to find her still struggling to get up. I calmed her down, gave her the injections, gave her more water, wetted her down with water, gave her more food, sprayed her with fly spray, and sat with her, stroking her and talking to her; waiting and praying for a miracle.

I couldn't sleep that night, worrying about her and wondering if she'd ever get up again. I went down to check on her several times during the night, and each time found her sleeping. Because she was so nearly deaf, she never heard me coming, and I was careful not to make enough noise to wake her. I figured the sleep would do her good after all she'd been through, and might even refresh her enough to give her the strength to get up on her own when the next day began.

I woke up early that next morning to find her still down. I called the vet and arranged for him to come later in the morning, and asked him to bring the drugs to euthanize her if he thought that there was no hope for her. My neighbor came over that morning and tried once more to get her up, but it was no use. He offered to come back and shoot her for me, but I couldn't stand the thought of a painful and violent death; most of her life had been filled with pain and mistreatment at human hands. If death was to come to her that morning, it was going to come gently, and with love.

After he left I sat down in front of her and stroked her beautiful face and looked into her eyes. I couldn't speak, and tears were streaming down my face. Our eyes locked, and I felt that I was looking into her soul, and I knew that she was seeing mine. The air stood still, the wind did not blow, there was no buzz of bee or fly that I was aware of; I was conscious only of the deep connection of our hearts and souls at that moment. I will never forget the power of those few minutes, when we wordlessly exchanged communication.

I told her I loved her, and that I didn't want her to go. I told her she had to try to get up, that it was her only hope. She let out a huge sigh, her eyes never leaving mine, and she told me that she couldn't get up. She wanted to, but she couldn't, and she told me that it was her time to go. I sobbed and cried "No," but I knew it was true.

I calmed down then, and went to get her some of her favorite treats. I came back and stayed with her until the vet came. He examined her and told me what I already knew— she was not able to get back up. I stayed with her while he injected the tranquilizer, then the euthanasia drug; I stroked her as she died quickly and quietly.

A Very
Special Teacher

JEAN M. FOGLE

Vicki Lutz opened the side door of her van and 11 eager dogs leaped out. Flip, the 12-year-old Dalmatian, was the last to exit. While the others demonstrated their agility, flyball and tetherball prowess, Flip waited patiently, tail wagging, for his turn to shine.

Flip demonstrated the principles of basic obedience, calmly obeying Lutz's commands. Afterwards, when she led Flip into the crowd, Lutz invited the children to greet him. As they gathered around to admire Flip's spotted coat, one child shouted: "Hey, Ms. Lutz! How can he jump? His eyes are sewn shut!"

Lutz, of Maurertown, Va., explained how glaucoma, a disease that increases pressure inside the eyeball, caused Flip to lose his vision in both eyes. Flip's job at this demonstration was to help spectators understand dogs can overcome disabilities and lead useful lives. The children learned to become more tolerant themselves as they watched the other dogs accept Flip. People of all ages flocked to the dashing Dalmatian wherever he went, and he returned everyone's affection with kisses.

When North Fork Middle School in Quicksburg, Va., was looking for new electives to offer students, Lutz, a physical-education teacher, suggested pet-care, and administrators said yes. Flip became one of the first canine teachers, going into classrooms every day for five years. He patiently allowed the students to groom his coat, demonstrated obedience and agility, and offered unconditional love. Flip's beautifully spotted coat drew children to him, but his winning disposition made many students fall in love with him. When the time came to choose dogs to work with in class, the kids always clamored to get Flip.

Lutz had always wanted a Dalmatian and knew Flip was the one for her. His personality was perfect and his puppy beauty irresistible. About a year and a half ago, she noticed that Flip's left eye looked cloudy. A veterinarian diagnosed him with glaucoma and referred him to Virginia Tech's veterinary clinic in Blacksburg, where doctors confirmed the diagnosis, removed the eyeball, replaced it with a prosthesis and stitched shut the eyelid. Afterward, it looked like he had one eye closed. Flip recovered quickly and went back to work.

One morning 13 months later, Lutz noticed Flip was not in his usual place on the couch. "When I saw him facing the wall, I had a bad feeling [about the other eye]," Lutz said. "Checking his eye, I could tell immediately his sight was gone. After the veterinarian removed the eye, he refused to eat. For three days he barely moved or responded to anything, and nothing I did comforted him. On the fourth day, just when I was beginning to despair, he got up and slowly made his way to the door. I knew then that he would be able to adjust.

"Flip was always a very independent dog," Lutz continued. "Coming when called depended on his mood. Being blind has changed that. He follows my voice everywhere and is content to be by my side."

Flip still goes to school as a guest teacher in the pet-care program. Instead of teaching agility and obedience, he teaches children about disabilities. "In our rural area, animals are often viewed as productive or nonproductive," said Tracy Phillips, a reading specialist at North Fork Middle School. "Animals less than perfect are often put to sleep. Seeing Flip as an active member of the community helps teach the students compassion. Even though Flip isn't perfect, the children see he is still able to make contributions to his family and others."

On weekdays, Flip spends a lot of time at home relaxing on the sofa. Lutz leaves the door cracked open so Flip can find his way to the yard, and he is happy awaiting the return of his family at the end of the day. At the demonstrations Lutz gives on weekends, Flip has many opportunities to be in the spotlight. Out in the sunshine with a crowd of admirers surrounding him, Flip wags his tail and shakes his beautiful body, eager to begin the next lesson.

from DOG FANCY

The Sound of Trouble's Sorrow

CAROLYN CAHILL

"Has anything changed at home that could be upsetting him?" the vet asked as he felt Trouble's belly, checking the severity of his urinary tract infection.

"Well . . . yes," I said. I was pleased that this doctor considered the physical manifestations of emotional unrest, an indication that he was empathetic, but I was hesitant to tell him what most people heard with difficulty. "Um-m, well, Alan recently had brain surgery. He lost the use of the right side of his body and he's in a wheelchair. I imagine the cats are upset by that."

The doctor continued palpating Trouble and extended his question as if he hadn't heard my answer. "Something along the lines of a change in the cat food he's getting, or if you've moved recently? Oh, well, sometimes we just don't know why these things happen."

But I knew. . . .

Sweetie and Trouble had been living with us for over a year before Alan was first diagnosed with brain cancer. We had adopted them when they were about a year old from my young niece and nephew who were moving overseas. It was a big decision for us; we were hesitant at first, wondering if the four of us could live comfortably in our small one-bedroom apartment in New York City, and if we wanted the responsibility. Our hesitation faded as our excitement rose, and totally left through the door when the cats arrived.

Within a few days they were right at home and we had fallen in love with them, delighting in our new family. They are very special cats, with strong personalities and a lot of life. Trouble, named for his mischievous nature as a kitten, is the larger of the two. He is heavy-set and all black except for a bit of white on his chin, belly and two front paws. He is the strong, silent type, demands affection when he feels like it (although is usually not in the mood) and is quite jealous of his sister who is far more affectionate by nature. Sweetie is a petite, gray tabby with a lot of white on her tummy and legs. She is quite active, a bit nervous, but very feminine, dainty and very, very sweet. Trouble and Sweetie made up for the small living quarters by running around our rooms over and over again, typically Sweetie being chased by Trouble, who was a bit of a bully.

It was over a year after they joined us that Alan was diagnosed with the brain tumor. After months of unsuccessful treatment he underwent surgery to resect as much of it as possible. But, as the doctors had feared, there were complications: he lost almost all use of the right side of his body and his speech was severely affected. The cancer was very aggressive; he was given less than a year to live.

After several long months in the hospital's rehabilitation center it was time for Alan to return home. He was excited about it, but there were lots of questions and some fears about reentering the "real world" in his new state of being. We wondered how he would manage to get around our small apartment in his wheelchair. He was also uncertain whether he wanted to keep the cats. He didn't want the added stress of worrying about running over tails or being jumped on when he wasn't in the mood. I left that decision to him and, thankfully, he eventually decided that he would enjoy their companionship.

Alan adjusted quickly to being at home, and although the cats were a bit wary of the wheelchair they were glad to see him. But they knew something was wrong. During this time Trouble the (sometimes) bully took on a new role as the wise and compassionate one. In the mornings he would leave his nighttime post at the foot of the bed to lie between us with his two little white paws resting gently on Alan's right arm, the arm that was damaged. He would just sit and stare at Alan very knowingly. Alan often remarked, "Look, Trouble's praying for me."

Typically animals help us to open our hearts as we care for them and love them. In this case Trouble was not looking to receive warmth or affection. He appeared to be there to comfort and thereby heal Alan, and he seemed to take this responsibility very seriously.

Alan had been home for several months, which were beautiful and often extremely difficult, when one morning, out of the blue, Trouble started acting strangely. He wouldn't eat, which was unusual, and just sat and hissed at nothing in particular, which was also odd, as I'd never heard him make a noise before. Luckily, there was a veterinarian's office in our building so I took him right in. I was thankful for the proximity of the office; if it had been anywhere else I would have had to wait for someone to come and stay with Alan, so I lost no time in getting Trouble the attention he needed. As we learned, Trouble had a urinary tract infection, which the vet said can be deadly in male cats if not treated right away.

The very next day I was back in the hospital, but this time it was the New York Hospital Emergency Room with Alan. It was a stressful 18+ hours of scans, procedures, and IV medication as the doctors tried to reduce the swelling in his brain caused by the chemotherapy treatment he was undergoing. Moderate success allowed us to return home.

It was less than two months later when Trouble was unwell again with the same symptoms as before. This time it was during the night and I had to bring him across town to an all-night animal hospital. Once again, within a few hours, Alan was rushed to the Emergency Room. This time, however, the doctors were unable to help him and we lost him.

Some people believe that through their devotion our animals often take on some of our suffering. I believe Trouble did this for Alan. In my mind it was no coincidence that the only times in his life that Trouble was sick and rushed to the hospital were directly preceding Alan getting sick and having to be rushed to the hospital.

The cats were used to Alan not being home, since during his eight months with cancer he spent many weeks in the hospital. But they sensed that this time his absence was different. For the first few mornings after Alan's passing, Trouble lay in Alan's empty spot on the bed and howled mournfully. It was a deeply sorrowful, primal yowl that seemed to emanate from a place well beyond his small feline body. I was startled, even a bit frightened for a moment, until I realized he was crying with me.

The sound of Trouble's sorrow was welcome reassurance that I was not alone in my mourning. We both had cared for

Alan in the best way we could, both had taken on as much
of his burden as we were able. And as the rest of the world
just kept going, business as usual, when friends and family put
on their brave faces and tried to urge my sadness away with
small talk and questions about the future, I was grateful to
have Trouble, who had no shame over mourning our tremendous loss.

Woe Be to Me

NANCY B. GIBBS

"Why, Lord?" I asked as I gazed toward the sky, laced with beautiful white clouds. I was feeling pretty low. My health was not the best it had ever been, and the grief of losing my father a few months earlier weighed heavily on my mind. I guess you could say I was experiencing a crippling "woe-be-to-me" attitude. My spirit needed lifting and my soul definitely could have used a little mending.

I decided that going out into God's beautiful world might help my overcast mood. The sunshine could bring a little life back into my spirit and the gentle breeze would probably be good for my soul.

A few tears fell down my cheeks as I sat quietly on my patio. I thought about how I had been a little impatient lately with some of the people I loved dearly. In addition to my broken spirit, I felt a sense of guilt, as well.

"We all need a little maintenance as we get older," my husband had whispered, trying to console me a few days earlier. "Once you get your medication regulated you'll be like new again."

As I gently rocked, I glanced over at my dog, Snowball. She was lying in the sunshine, absorbing God's gift of warmth. I remembered her health problems over the years and thanked

God that she was still alive. At thirteen years old, her eyesight was gone and her hearing was gradually fading away. Snowball's life had never been easy. She had fought many diseases. As a tiny puppy, she was not expected to live after a bout of distemper. A few years later, spinal meningitis almost took her away from us. After two rounds of heartworm treatments, she fought hard. Snowball was determined to live, despite the odds, which were against her.

Despite the fact that she has been very sick over the years, and that she has become blind and almost deaf in her old age, she continues to be happy to be alive. Fortunately, she knows her way around her backyard. She knows exactly where to find her house, her feeding bowl and the water bucket. Just a pat on her head makes her wiggle with delight. For a few kind words, she gives me that doggy smile that has always melted my heart. She is never impatient with me. She seems to value each day of her life and lives it to the fullest, even in the confines of her unfocused world. She always looks forward to the few minutes of love that I give her each day.

"Why can't I be more like Snowball?" I wondered.

Compared to Snowball's problems, my trials are few. While Snowball's world is confined to her small backyard, I am free to explore the world around me. I can physically see the beauty of the earth. Snowball can only see the sights that remain in her memory banks and hear the extra-loud sounds around her.

"I love you, girl," I whispered, as I walked over to Snowball and patted her head. She wagged her tail and crawled into my lap. She reached up and gently licked my face. My soul was slowly being mended and my spirits raised.

I discovered that it doesn't take perfect health to be happy.

It does take an attitude adjustment, at times. My "woe-be-to-me" attitude was quickly being transformed into a spirit of gratitude for the gifts God has given to me. The first thing for which I thanked Him was my friend, Snowball, and the message of joy she shared with me that Sunday afternoon.

DON'T BE AFRAID

---

*"I will strengthen thee; yea,
I will help thee. . . ."*

ISAIAH 41:10, KJV

---

*H*ave you ever noticed that animals don't seem to worry about tomorrow? They live in the here and now. And they enjoy it. They seem to know that God will be there for us in all of our tomorrows—that he will give us the strength we need to solve our problems and deal with our crises.

How comforting it is to have them near us when our world is a little shaken. They remind us that God is near—always.

Alberta

LONNIE HULL DuPONT

It was on the first of May that my husband Joe and I heard the strange noises from under the yew bushes next to our patio. It was a lovely spring day, the day before my stepfather's birthday—the man who raised me and had died only three months before.

This was a noise we didn't know, being city folk who'd moved to the country. Joe peered through the bushes. "It's a chicken," he announced.

"A chicken?" I found this hard to believe. Yes, we lived in the country, but there were no chickens in the immediate vicinity.

"It's little and black," he added. "Should we feed it?"

"I don't know what chickens eat," I said. I knew they liked to pick things off the ground, but that was about it. I went indoors and rustled up some unsalted peanuts and unpopped popcorn, and the hen did indeed come forth and eat.

We sat and watched her. She was tiny, raven black, with a deep red comb which extended in red leathery seams into her face. I've never been one to notice chickens particularly, but we both agreed she was very pretty.

And hungry. And noisy. She clucked away and looked at us and waddled around us as we sat on the patio. We decided to name her Alberta after my stepdad Al, not only because his birthday was the following day but also because he had bought his first Model T with a box of banty hens. And because he would not eat poultry.

I figured somehow Alberta had wandered off from her farm and that she would return to it. I didn't expect her to be with us the next day. But there she was, sitting quietly on the patio, waiting to be fed. I called my sister and brother-in-law to ask about proper food, and they supplied us with a big bag of chicken feed.

In the meantime, I was immersed in a fairly severe depression. Many months later I would learn it was from a physical ailment, and I am now in successful treatment for that illness. But at the time, I decided that I would try gardening to help my state of mind. I kept it simple, buying only a few things at the nursery. But the initial planting seemed overwhelming. That week I sat down on the patio steps and began to cry.

I sensed a little presence at my feet. I opened my eyes and there stood Alberta, cocking her head at me. She had food. She was standing near me because she wanted to. I started that day a tradition of talking to her as if she could understand me. I came to believe God had sent her to me.

The initial work of putting in the garden was too much for me at that time, so I hired a couple of college guys to help. Alberta joined us in our work. Every time the guys dug a worm up, they'd toss it to her, and she caught it mid-air. She ate well that day. And now I had a garden where Alberta and I could putter.

I don't know a lot about chickens. Maybe they're all this sociable. But Alberta loved to hang around people. We had my mother's 80th birthday party on the patio a week after Alberta's arrival, and that morning Joe raked up winter's leftovers for three hours. Alberta followed him around, sometimes perching on the yew bushes, sometimes bobbing contentedly nearby in the grass. When the guests arrived, she mingled, a complete hit. Everyone fell in love with her.

All summer Alberta stayed. We fed and watered her and found her eggs here and there. Although the side patio and its yew bushes were her home, if we missed a feeding or were too late, she would walk around the house, up the steps, and cluck up such a racket at the front door that our housecat was simply beside herself. And Alberta would get her breakfast, pronto.

Both Joe and I found ourselves talking to her. She was almost eating out of Joe's hand. I would often sit on the patio steps and watch her edge closer to me, yet keep a little distance. I cooed over her, told her my problems. I prayed while sitting out there, so grateful was I that this little bird came along to distract me from my darkness.

This part of Michigan has coyotes and any number of other wild things that could hurt her. But she stayed safe. Nevertheless, we knew that when cold weather hit, she could not survive without shelter. So we put the word out: Would someone like a pet hen and not eat her?

Someone would. My niece and her family lived about ten miles away and were willing to take her to add to their growing menagerie. We really didn't want her to go, but we knew it was necessary. It was now the end of summer, and I was on the mend. Still, I hated to let my little bird go.

On the last day, we sat outside and told Alberta where she was going and why. We put some feed in the bottom of a laundry basket on its side. She waddled around it, then walked in and began to eat. We slowly righted the basket and put a lid on it, then drove to my niece's. Sure enough, there were pets galore; in particular, one fat friendly hen named Goldilocks who would become Alberta's best friend.

Today Alberta runs around a big back yard with Goldilocks. Their wings are unclipped so they can fly from danger, and they lay eggs wherever they wish. At night the two of them roost in a shed protected by a noisy billygoat who really likes them. I expect Alberta to live a long healthy life.

As for me, I'm back to myself. The world is a wonderful place again for me. I continue in the knowledge that God made the creatures of the earth for very good reasons. And I believe in particular that he created a lovely banty hen and delivered her to me to get me through that summer. I will be forever grateful.

Shadow & Soul

T. J. BANKS

I am sitting at my word processor, staring tiredly at the lines on the screen. Words that were flame-vivid to me just a short time before now feel lifeless: I've lost the magic, that sense of being spellbound by my fictional dream. I push my chair back and wonder why I sit alone in this room, day after day, trying to weave all these words and images together. Then I hear a "Miaow-ow" and feel a paw on my shoulder. I turn my head slightly, and there is Cricket, balancing on her back paws, ballerina-style, on the edge of the desk behind me. She stares at me, her amber eyes large and anxious. Then she jumps down from the desk, scurries over to my worktable, and makes a bold leap for kitty-kind onto the top of the monitor. She dangles her velvety white paws over the screen and gazes at me, purring. I am no longer alone. I scritch her ears, play with her front paws a bit, and start typing again.

Cats and writing go together for me: both have been a part of my life for as long as I can remember. Writing is a lonely, demanding business, and cats are especially good at supplying the quiet companionship—*and* comic relief—that we writers need so badly. All seven of our cats are curious about the word processor, but Cricket, chief editor-cat, regards it as her particular property. Back when she was a runty, big-eared, grayish-brown tiger kitten, she used to make a point of sitting on my lap while I was typing, her eyes lighting up as she pressed one key after another. Or all of them at once. My husband Tim and I would make jokes about the book she was trying to write. I had more typos than usual in my stories and articles, but Cricket seemed satisfied with the results.

Nowadays she's mostly content to stretch out on the floor or on the printer while I work, waiting for me to take a break and drag her long-tailed catnip critters around for her. The best editors, she clearly believes, should know enough to kick back during the creative process.

I think of her as my soul because sometimes she reads me better than I do. Cricket senses when I'm lonely or just plain having a case of the writer's blues. She stays with me then, rubbing her face against mine and making little concerned noises. She'll curl up in my lap or on the table next to me, one white-gloved paw curled around my finger, and purr until my dark mood passes. At night, she snuggles up close to me, *squunking* happily. (A *squunk* is somewhere between a purr and a sigh, and it's the most contented, soothing noise, especially on those nights when my chronic insomnia is winning the war.)

Cricket and Tikvah (which is Hebrew for "hope") are inseparable in my mind—partly because they look so much alike and partly because they both have needed so much more love and reassurance than the other cats. Cricket, the runt of the litter, had, and still has, a strong need to be stroked and held. Tikvah, a former stray, still carries the emotional scars of that life and is easily startled or frightened. Tim calls her "a big complex with claws," and there's more than a little truth to the description.

Tikvah was living out in my mom's field with a single look-alike kitten when I first saw her. Something about the sight of *this* mom fending for her kitten and herself caught at my cat-susceptible heart, and I instinctively started putting food out for them. The kitten either died or took off on its own after a few months; but Tikvah kept coming around, torn between her desire for food and affection and her fear of people. After awhile, she'd let me stroke her head; if I tried to pick her up, however, she'd struggle, her double-paws flailing every which way. So I learned to wait and let her come to me.

One day, about seven months after she started showing up for meals, Tim and I caught her and brought her home with us. She was sick. Very sick. Her light-gray fur with the darker gray stripes and soft orange shadings—kitty highlights, I suppose you could call those touches of orange scattered throughout her thick coat—was dull and lifeless; so were her large, green, owl eyes. She had worms, cystitis, and bronchitis so severe, it sounded as if she were about to rip apart at the seams every time she coughed.

She was not, Tim insisted, going to live with us: we already had three cats at the time, and I couldn't keep giving in to what he called my "Mother Teresa complex" whenever a homeless feline came my way. So I made a few efforts to place her, but my heart wasn't in it. I couldn't think about letting Tikvah go to anyone, friend or stranger without feeling horribly guilty. In her own funny, hesitant way, she'd begun to trust me; and giving her away would've been a breaking of that trust. Then, too, Tikvah was such a nervous, defensive cat, I was afraid very few people would put up for long with the way she had of suddenly, unexpectedly striking out with those extra claws of hers.

Of course, she ended up staying with us. She already had

me smack in the middle of her very capable double-paws; and Tim, despite all his talk, was as much of a mush about cats as I was. So she lucked out, as our vet, Tom, told her. Or, as Rod, an old bus driver friend of mine, put it when I told him Tikvah's story and what her name meant, "Because she *had* hope." I started to say no, that wasn't quite it—we'd named her "Tikvah" because she'd *needed* hope—but then stopped myself. Because I suddenly saw that Rod *was* right—"Tikvah" had been the right name for her because she had had hope come to her in the form of two off-beat, cat-crazed humans who didn't know how to walk away and leave "well enough" alone.

For her, it was like having a second chance at kittenhood. She had food and stand-up radiators and even a waterbed to snooze on (although even now, when she hears a thunderstorm or even a good, fierce wuthering wind, she'll wake up out of a sound sleep, her green eyes wide with fear and remembering). She had toys, which she hoarded happily under the coffee table. She even had other cats to hang out with, once she felt less threatened by them. Tikvah wasn't too sure about us, though. She liked being petted, yes; but she'd also learned at some point in her previous life that human hands could hurt you, and she was wary.

Two years and a lot of love and patience later, Tikvah has finally begun to trust us. Sometimes she still claws and nips when she really means to nuzzle or play. And she still gets frightened if Tim or I try to pick her up. But she shadows me around the house a good part of the day and evening and constantly butts her head against our hands for attention. She has even become a snuggler—on her own terms. If I am lying quietly on the sofa under her favorite afghan, she'll hop up and stretch out full-length alongside or on top of me. If I move, even if it's just the tiniest fraction, she'll jump down and scurry out of the room.

If Cricket is my soul, then Tikvah is my shadow, and not just because of the way she trails me about. She is my shadow-self, the fearful one in each of us that wants to trust but pulls back, remembering past hurts and bruises. She has taught me that trust—whether it's the trust of a human who finds it hard to let his soul-wounds heal or of a stray cat who has never known gentleness or love before—comes even more slowly and silently than Carl Sandburg's cat-footed fog. That it involves holding one's self still—and listening.

Two Gray Doves

ANNE WATKINS

If ever I needed a sign from God, it was during the summer of 1995. I'd been the victim of a vicious physical assault a couple of years earlier and had finally managed to piece my shattered life back together, thanks to the love and support of my husband and daughter. There had been a police investigation, grand jury testimony, and lots of meetings with lawyers. The court system can be agonizingly slow, as I found out. But now all the waiting was over and the trial was set to start within the week.

My job helped keep my mind off things, but the closer the trial date got, the more my tightly stretched nerves jangled. I wasn't looking forward to being in court—I would have to face my attacker for the first time since the incident and I wasn't sure if I could handle it. Then, early that week, as I stepped outside to go to work, something caught my eye and diverted my attention.

Two gray doves circled the yard, did some incredibly fancy acrobatics, then landed on a power line over my house. They rested there, gazing calmly back at me, as I stared up at them. Doves aren't unheard of in our rural part of the country, but they don't usually put on such a show! I didn't know why, but a tiny bit of hope tip-toed in among the black web of fear that had strangled my thoughts. The image of those two doves kept circling back to nudge my thoughts as I went about my work that day. There was something about them. . . .

The next day was the first day of the trial. With trembling hands I dressed, did my hair and tried to get some breakfast down. My husband smiled reassuringly at me and said, "I'll be right there. Everything is going to be okay."

I smiled back, but the awful tightness of my throat made my voice a weak croak when I tried to respond. We embraced, then stepped out the front door together.

There they were again! The same two gray doves I'd seen the day before. Once more, they cavorted and cartwheeled and performed dazzling aerial stunts before alighting on the power lines near our house. They rested a moment, then took off again, putting on an impressive display that rivaled any air show I had ever seen.

We watched in amazement. As the birds flew loops overhead, some of the fear in my soul began melting away. Finally the doves settled on the lines again and we got into the car. As we drove away, I glanced back at them. A soft sensation of peace was gently stealing into my heart. Maybe this whole mess wouldn't be so bad after all.

But on the way to the courthouse I found myself battling waves of nausea and the old familiar demon of terror. My family would be in the courtroom with us. They hadn't heard all the awful details of the attack. It would be so horrible for them and they had already suffered enough. And what would I do when the perpetrator stared me in the eye? Would I be able to handle it? Then another thought crept in, just a tiny whisper, really: "What if he pleads guilty?"

The moment that thought crossed my mind, all feelings of dread and anguish abruptly vanished. It was as if someone had wrapped a warm blanket of love and comfort around my shoulders. That one little thought . . . I felt as though I could face anything. The sweet sensation of calmness stayed with me as we entered the courtroom and watched the lawyers hurry about, preparing to begin the trial.

The one I had dreaded facing sat across the room, glaring at me. My investigator sat down beside me and whispered, "Don't look at him. He's trying to intimidate you."

I kept my gaze focused firmly on the table before me but I could feel the man's dark eyes boring into me. The image of the doves came back and I smiled to myself. Everything would be okay, one way or another. Then my lawyer approached the table and motioned for us to join him in a side room. My husband slipped his hand into mine as we went. Suddenly, my heart crammed itself painfully into my throat. What did this mean?

Closing the door, the attorney turned to face me, then broke into a huge smile. "He pled guilty," he told us. "There won't be a trial."

I felt as light as those two doves that had visited us that morning! It literally felt as if a physical weight had been lifted off my shoulders. All the way home my husband and I rejoiced. I couldn't wait to see those doves circling our house again. I wanted to thank them for their encouragement.

I watched for them for days, then for weeks. They never came back, or if they did, they never made themselves visible. And even though I haven't seen their graceful acrobatics since, I will always feel their presence in my heart.

A Jingle of Praise

DIANE M. CIARLONI

His voice was soft, gentle and far too small to belong to the body that housed it. The sound that rippled across his vocal cords came as a surprise, rather like a very large man speaking in a falsetto. But, really, it was difficult to gauge the true proportions of his body. It appeared as if it *should* be large, but it was too thin to make an accurate determination. Ribs were plainly visible on both sides. Hip bones protruded like miniature hat racks. The feet were big. His eyes, or what I could see of them, were dull from lack of food and general care. The hair was lackluster, as if barely hanging on to life. Still, there was a strange feeling that a bed of embers, ready to ignite, rested under the surface.

His hair was his most arresting feature. It was the color of a fading sunset. I'd seen that same tint sweep across the California desert sky. Not yellow. Not orange. Somewhere between those two strong extremes. The only word offering a somewhat appropriate description was gold. Pale gold. Golden. In this case, standing so that he was backlit by the sun, the ends of the softly golden hair seemed dipped in something translucent . . . opalescent, perhaps.

He turned ever so slightly and provided me with the full benefit of his stare. That's when I saw that the color of his eyes was less than two shades darker than his hair. He was almost a monochromatic gold.

He was going to "speak." I could tell by the barely percep-tible movement of his mouth, offering just a hint of separation between his top and bottom teeth. I waited. He never moved his eyes from mine.

Meo-r-r-r-owat?

This was no ordinary cat meow. The gaunt, golden feline seemed to sing with an odd sweetness that was in jarring juxta-position to his physical condition.

Meo-r-r-r-owat?

I'd watched those late-night television shows with their alleged talking animals, and even sat through those so-called funny videos with yodeling dogs, but never, until this instant, had I been confronted with an actual talking cat. There was no mistaking the word. He was looking at me and asking, *"What?"*

"What?" I queried back. "You showed up at my house, so why are you asking *me* 'what'?"

The golden cat never twitched a muscle. His appearance said he'd probably been dumped into the woods behind my house at least a month ago, roaming and foraging on what birds and mice he could snare.

"This is crazy," I said to myself. "This cat and I have been staring at one another for 15 minutes. Somebody needs to do something."

I sighed and turned for the house. I knew my husband would be aggravated over the possibility of yet another cat to add to our already huge collection of canines, felines, birds and rabbits; and I also knew I was already well beyond the allow-able number of pets as laid out in our town ordinance. Still, there was no way I'd turn away an animal and, first things first, this one needed food.

My hand was on the door when he spoke again.

Meo-r-r-owat?

I turned, smiling. "What I'm doing is getting food for you," I answered. I knew he understood. He was emaciated and unkempt but, unexplainably, his compelling dignity was intact. I could see it in the lift of his head and the controlled curve of his spine.

I took my hand from the doorknob and made a complete pivot to face the cat. I knew he was probably wary, but I decided to attempt some physical contact before getting the food. It was the reverse of my usual process with strays, but I squatted down with maybe ten feet separating us.

"Kitty, kitty, kitty," I called. Even if I live to be one hundred, I'll never unravel the great mystery of the universe which asks: Why does every cat in the world answer to "kitty, kitty"? Not one dog in the entire country will even think about breaking stride for some silly person standing there and calling, "Here doggie, doggie, doggie." The cat didn't come, but neither did he run.

By now the sun was shifting its light away from the cat's back. His hair lost some of the translucent tinge, but the color still brought to mind a late afternoon desert mirage. Shimmering. As we stared at one another, I remembered a legend I'd come across during research for a book. It said southern plantations welcomed the sight of a golden cat since it signaled the promise of coming prosperity. As lovely as he was, I didn't think this particular golden cat would do much to relieve the financial and emotional problems I'd labored under for so long. Unpaid bills. Car needing repair. Stress and strain in my marriage.

Meo-r-r-owat?

I shook my head. It was uncanny. I wondered if he could say anything else. This time, I took the single word as an invitation to approach. I did, slowly. The cat never moved. I stretched out my hand and laid it gently behind his head, stroking down his back. I could feel all the knobs and ridges along his backbone, and with it came a sense of instantaneous anger for the person who could allow this to happen to one of God's creatures. Then the cat looked at me and, somehow, I knew anger was inappropriate. It wasn't what he wanted.

"You need a name," I said to him. Uh-oh. That meant I'd already made up my mind to keep the golden cat.

I looked at him and, suddenly, a word popped into my brain. "Jingle!" I said it with a sense of excitement. "I have no idea why, but you're supposed to be Jingle." I went inside to get what would be the first of many meals for him.

Jingle required no adjustment period. He just, well, he just *was.* His settling in was so solid that it seemed he'd always been there. He wasn't a bully but neither did he back down from anyone. It was obvious he preferred to settle problems and differences through considerate negotiations. And, whatever happened, he never lost his dignity. Just a few days after he arrived, one of the other cats, Doso, approached him with a determined look in his eyes. His intention was to drive Jingle on his way. He arched his back. Jingle didn't budge. Doso moved closer and then leaped. Jingle, in one fluid movement, wound his body out of the way and, without breaking stride, raised one paw and delivered a swift swipe across the nose. That ended the situation. Doso was convinced. Not one growl had escaped Jingle's mouth. He never raised his voice. He simply dealt with the problem and then moved on to more pleasant things.

The golden cat ate and gained weight. His entire body became larger, with all the parts and their proportions in lovely symmetry with one another. I bought him a leather collar with a bell stitched to the center. Now he jingled when he walked, lending a sense of alliteration to his name.

Somehow, without either of us doing anything intentional, Jingle became a special source of comfort for me. The times were hard, and every day seemed punctuated with its own particular brand of emotional anguish. For long stretches of day after day I was unable to feel the presence of God. I didn't—couldn't—pray. The words were damned up somewhere deep down, and I couldn't find the key to unlock the door holding them prisoner. But every day, usually several times each day, I talked with Jingle.

One morning I padded barefoot to the upstairs balcony, finding Jingle curled on the cushions of the wicker sofa. His eyes were wide open. It wasn't daylight but he, too, was awake. I sat down next to him.

Meo-r-r-owat? he asked.

"You know what it is," I answered as I began patting and scratching him.

No-o-ow, he responded.

I smiled at him. "Now?" I asked. "You just said 'now'?" Suddenly something happened. The dam broke. The words tumbled over one another without conscious thought as I stroked and scratched the golden cat.

"Bless You, Lord," I almost sobbed. "Thank You for blessing me with this cat. You're wonderful and loving and kind and forgiving. You send me new mercy every day. You renew my anointing. You remind me that You understand me because wasn't it You who made my heart? You know me, love me and understand me even when I don't understand myself. Thank You for Your grace and Your mercy."

The words were a constant stream, not stopping until I left Jingle and returned to the house.

It became a ritual. I would stroke Jingle and praise the Lord. It was beyond my understanding. Finally, I called a friend and explained the situation to her.

"The Lord is good," she said. "He knew your problems, so He sent a way for you to talk to Him. He knew you could relate to Jingle. He didn't want you to stay away from Him so He created a door for you to walk through." He truly can make a way where there is no way.

Before too much time passed, I was again able to pray on my own; but that didn't stop the instantaneous praise that began every time my fingers ran across Jingle's sun-tipped, golden hair.

That all happened 12 years ago. I frequently squint my eyes when I look at Jingle. I keep thinking he must surely be growing older and slowing down. But, strangely, it isn't happening. Even my husband marvels over the way he still scales a tree or leaps across a stream in the woods. All of his vitality—and all of his dignity—are still intact.

Just as the old legend said, the golden cat did bring great prosperity with him; but he deposited it in my heart rather than in my bank account.

The Education of Pinkie

THIRZA PEEVEY

When I was living in another state, I broke driving horses and taught people to drive. I received a call one day from a young woman who had a pony she wanted to break to drive, I'll call her Jan.* I agreed to meet her at her mother's farm and look at the pony.

Accordingly, a few days later I stopped by the farm and tried out the pony. Someone else had already started the thirteen-hand palomino mare, but had quit after ground-driving and getting her used to harness. The trainers had done a good job, and I said so. I felt we could finish it in a matter of days.

After looking at the pony, Jan took me to the house to meet her mother. Mother was out walking through her yard and came to greet us. The strength of her character and her confidence was evident in the way she carried herself and in the short, declarative sentences she used. You could tell she wasn't used to argument or nonsense. She didn't like excuses from others and she didn't accept them from herself. She was a lovely woman in her fifties, with piercing blue eyes. Her hand-

---

*Names have been changed to protect the privacy of the people in the story.

shake was firm and strong and her posture upright, despite the fact that she was recuperating from a broken back. She'd been master of foxhounds at a local hunt club and had an unfortunate accident.

"It wasn't Kit's fault," she explained as we chatted. "She was always an honest mare. She just wasn't strong enough for the jump. I should have known better." There was a terrible jump behind the club in the woods. The jumping panel itself was a hog fence. A hog fence is a split rail fence made tight enough for pigs. Two posts are mounted side by side where one would normally be sunk. Then rails are stacked between the posts instead of being placed in mortises in the post. The unfortunate thing for Kit is that you can't see through a hog fence, as there was a stream on the other side of this one. Beyond the stream, there was just one stride and then you had to make a hard turn to avoid crashing into the woods.

"Kit always threw everything into a jump. She knew she couldn't do this one when she got into the middle of it and saw the stream, but it was too late. She tried to throw herself back, but the momentum was all forward and she crashed. She wasn't hurt, but my back was broken," Mother continued. "I had the best orthopedist in the state, and he saved my ability to walk, but I'll never ride again." Her voice was steady and strong, but you could see the sadness in her eyes when she said it.

"I've never been without a horse before," she offered. "My father bred steeplechasers on the farm where I grew up. I had a pony from the time I could walk. I rode out with him from the time I was a tiny child, and we always hunted. Some of the best 'chasers ever, came out of our barn." I couldn't help but notice the concern with which Jan watched her mother as she spoke.

When we finished chatting, we set up a schedule to work the pony and agreed that they would send their hired man to pick up my wagon so we could use it with "Pinkie." I headed home.

A few days later, we met at the barn to begin the final stages of breaking Pinkie. I spent an afternoon ground-driving with the harness on, just to get used to the pony. The next session we began pulling the wagon around behind her. In a week's time, she was used to the wagon and we hooked her to it. A few more days and we were driving on the farm roads. Pinkie took to her new line of work with gusto.

Next we turned to the tasks of getting a suitable carriage and teaching Jan to drive. The carriage was easily accomplished. One trip to the Amish country in Pennsylvania and we found a lovely little Meadowbrook cart. It was well-built, light and well-balanced. Not perfect, but it made a good beginner's piece. As the original Meadowbrook was designed for older folks to hilltop, or follow the hounds from afar, it would be perfect for Jan's hunting interests. It could not be easily upset, it could handle rough off-road conditions and it was as safe as driving gets. Pinkie took to it well, and didn't even mind the switch from strictly pulling, with a wagon, to bearing part of the load, with a cart.

The next part wasn't so easily accomplished. Jan didn't seem to want to drive. She faithfully brought her small son to play with grandmother every day so she could take lessons from me. She paid attention while I explained maintenance of the cart and harness. She watched while I showed her how to safely harness the pony and put her to the cart. She listened when I explained how to adjust the harness and how to hold the lines. Try as I would, I couldn't get her to drive. She explained that she'd rather watch a pro do it.

I was confused. I didn't intend to drive for her forever. I was a teacher, not a professional coachman. I continued to try to coax her to take the lines all summer. Pinkie was, by this time, becoming quite the finished driving pony. She was calm and obedient in all situations. She could handle the cart in all types of terrain. She was well balanced and confident. She could muscle the cart around and put it exactly where she needed it to be. I had taught her to pull and hold back. We had encountered traffic, dogs and deer. Even school buses didn't bother her. I should have been long gone to my next client.

Then Jan stopped calling. "Well, I guess she didn't really want to drive," I thought. "That happens sometimes. Maybe it wasn't what she thought it would be." I put it out of my mind and started looking for a new student.

A few days later, I got a call from Mother. "My daughter doesn't want to drive anymore," she said. "I never could abide a horse just standing in the barn. Do you want to go driving?"

That was when I realized how clever Jan was. The pony was never for her. It was for her mother. Jan knew that her mother would never agree to driving lessons after a whole lifetime of riding and that horrifying accident. But she did know that her mother couldn't stand to see a horse going to waste. She had invested a considerable amount of money and six months of lessons to create a safe animal for her mother. Then she dropped it as a child casts away a toy, knowing that it would annoy Mother into driving.

Jan never drove the pony again. Mother and I, however, became fast friends. We drove that pony nearly every day, until Mother became a better whip than I. I moved away after two years of driving together, and Pinkie died a few years later of founder brought on by a metabolic problem. Mother, however, has been driving daily for thirteen years and is on her third pony now. Jan and Pinky gave her back the avocation that she loved. She still drives nearly every day on the roads and paths that wind through the hunt country she loves. In the summer, she occasionally hilltops in the early morning while the huntsman and the whips lead the young pups and young horses on their first cub hunts. In the fall, she goes to the meets in the afternoon to see the real hunts off. Every horse in the area has to be broke to the sight of a pony and carriage, as you never know when you will encounter Mother and her pony busily clipping along on the road or in the orchard and loving every minute of it.

LET ME HELP YOU

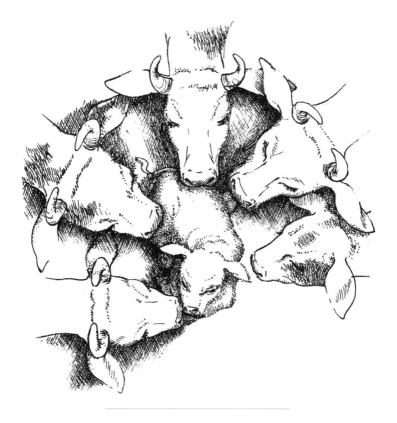

"When we give animals the opportunity, they can reach into our painful, hurt places and mend and soothe."

SUSAN CHERNAK McELROY

My dog Suzy likes to carry things in her mouth, and one of her greatest pleasures is to walk down to the road with me in the morning and carry our newspaper back to our house. One Sunday morning the newspaper was so thick that I thought it was too much for her and carried it myself. Halfway up the driveway, Suzy stopped and looked up at me with a hurt expression in her eyes. She wanted the newspaper. She wanted to help me, and she didn't care how heavy the burden was. So I gave her the newspaper and she carried it home with her head held high.

It wasn't the newspaper that mattered so much. Suzy just wants to help me carry any of my burdens. Animals are like that.

Misty and His Guardian Angel

GAY L. BALLIET

As we had many times before, we pulled up alongside Fred and Leah Sigley's—our neighbors—barn, and I jumped out first and ran inside. A sudden rustling came from the darkened box stall. Peering into the gloom, I was aware of the barn's musty smell: a mousy fume mixing with the sweet fragrance of grain and hay. Turning over and over in the straw, the pony writhed from the sharp pains of colic. With every violent roll, a new wave of barn scents drifted ominously.

We humans usually sense danger through our eyes and ears. We can sometimes see an automobile accident about to happen or hear a strong wind threatening to topple a tree. We can recognize approaching disaster listening to an argument between friends or hearing an explosion. But we seldom *smell* danger. It was through the sense of smell, however, that I could feel more poignantly a strange, even eerie, anxiety about this pony's condition. The pony, tossing in the straw from side to side to relieve the pain, roiled up odors sharper and more pungent from the rending. And there was a foreboding, an unexplainable apprehension about this bubbling cauldron of smells. I was used to the quiet odors of a barn, not a fulmination of them.

The dapple gray Shetland pony became still when the lights were flicked on. Leah and Edgar walked into the stable. The petite, short-haired, middle-aged woman with a thin-lipped smile stepped beside me and gripped the stall door's edge.

"Misty started rolling again," I said with worry, my gaze following the prostrate pony.

"I know; he's been doing that on and off all evening. I'm sorry to get you guys out here again tonight, but he doesn't seem to be able to shake this colic." Leah's forehead wrinkled into a frown, and she bit her lip. She continued, "Misty's not young, but we can't let anything happen to him because of Trudy. Trudy will die if anything happens to her little pony."

With a grim expression Edgar unlatched the stall door and stepped inside. Misty raised his head from the straw bed and stared.

"It's all right, Misty. I'm just here to help you." He patted the pony's side, bathed in sweat, and held the stethoscope to his flank. "Just want to listen to your gut, old boy," Edgar said in a low deliberate voice. The pony sank his tired head into the straw. Edgar moved the stethoscope from point to point, listening for the gut sounds that meant recovery. If he heard nothing, it meant there was a blockage, and unless the Sigleys agreed to surgery, death was almost a guarantee. He listened intently, his eyes focused on the cobwebs in the rafters.

Awaiting the verdict, Leah clenched the stall door. The pony's condition had deteriorated since we had seen him earlier.

Yesterday, after receiving a frantic call from Leah Sigley that something was wrong with Misty, we hurried to the farm. We had peered into the stall at Misty who, while not eating, was at least on his feet. Although he was kicking at his belly, it seemed like only a mild case of colic that a few shots of painkiller and an anti-spasmodic would cure.

Little Trudy Sigley, the Sigley's five-year-old daughter, had stood brushing her pony, telling it to "whoa" as Edgar made his initial examination of the animal. Her blonde curly head reached just about up to the pony's shoulder. An adorable girl with smooth, chubby pink cheeks, she brushed Misty all over with a soft body brush. Her hand barely fit around the brush, it was so small. Her full attention was on that pony, and the two looked a couple meant for each other, the one standing obediently while the other whisked little brush strokes all over his body.

"What's wrong with Mithty?" Trudy asked her mother, her eyebrows knitted into a Shirley Temple frown.

"He has a little bellyache, Trudy, that's all," her mother reassured. "Just hold him nice for Dr. Balliet so he doesn't walk away." The pony, so docile, wasn't even thinking of moving, but Trudy felt important and helpful holding him for Edgar. A cat jumped up to the stall ledge, and Trudy scolded it for intruding.

"You're a good nurse," Edgar said to the five-year-old as he injected banamine, a painkiller, into the vein. The pony didn't even jerk his head when the needle hit home.

"Thank you," Trudy said.

"Would you like to be a nurse when you get big?"

"No," she responded in a loud voice. "When I get big, I'm going to be a cowgirl."

"A cowgirl! That sounds exciting!" Edgar smiled. "I bet you and Misty will make a great team." Leah laughed and reminded Trudy to hold onto her pony real tight so that Dr. Balliet could give him another shot. The little girl planted her cowboy-booted feet squarely in the straw, and the small chubby fingers gripped tighter on his halter.

"Is he real sick?" Trudy asked, chewing her lower lip.

"No, he's sick, but not *real* sick," her mother said.

"Will I be able to ride him tomorrow?"

"Maybe, but I think we ought to give him a rest for a while, don't you? You know how you feel when you get sick. You just want to stay in bed and watch television."

"Can we bring in the television for Mithty, too?"

Edgar laughed and put the last syringe in his pocket. Her mother said, "No. Misty doesn't like television—except for westerns. Besides, he doesn't like all the commercials."

"Yuck, I don't blame you, Misty," Edgar agreed, patting the gray pony's neck. "Looks like you'll be up and trotting around in no time; then you can go outside and play."

"Will he be okay?" Trudy asked again. She stood on tiptoe and kissed the pony on the muzzle. He nuzzled and nudged her.

"Yes, he should be just fine in a day or two." Edgar straightened Trudy's cowgirl hat.

"Thank Dr. Balliet for coming out to check Misty this evening, Trudy," said Mrs. Sigley.

"Thank you for checking Mithty, Dr. Belly," Trudy said shyly, letting go the pony and following Edgar to the truck.

And with the cool September wind to our backs, we climbed into the truck. "That medication should take care of his problem, Leah. Keep an eye on him. If he gets worse, just give me a call."

As we had driven down the lane, the barn lights flicked off, and the rays from the outside lamp silhouetted the mother and daughter walking hand in hand back to the house.

A voice jolted me out of my recollection of the day before.

It was Edgar. "No gut motility now. Last night his guts were quite active, and he was gassy; now I hear nothing." Edgar was chewing a piece of straw, and his expression was grim. I knew what was coming next. "Doesn't look good, Leah. He's starting to dehydrate. It really doesn't look too good—sorry."

Leah's voice came in spurts, and she gripped the edge of Misty's stall so hard that her knuckles grew shiny white. "My God, what do I tell Trudy? That pony is the most important thing in her life. I don't know what I'll do if I have to tell her Misty will die," she fretted, wringing her hands. "How will I tell her?"

Edgar counseled, "Don't tell her yet, not if you don't have to. I'm going to pump everything I know of into this little guy." He thought. "First, we'll need to put him on IV fluids to take care of the dehydration." Determined, he went to the truck.

The night flowed into the barn and with it the frosty, moist September air. It was 12:30, and all was silent except for the hooting of a barn owl somewhere in the trees. Leah and I stepped outside, needing a reprieve from the grip of death.

A thin voice broke the silence in the stable behind us. "What's wrong with Mithty?" Startled, Leah and I turned, facing Trudy who we thought was asleep in the house. Her blonde hair was tousled, and her cotton nightie, with tiny blue flowers on a white background, was twisted between her legs. Her eyes were wide, and this time they demanded an honest answer.

"Trudy," her mother scolded, "What are you doing?"

"What's wrong with Mithty?" Trudy said again, running over to the stall in her bare feet. Her little face twitched as she saw our expressions.

You can never really trick children unless they allow you to.

Did my parents really think that I believed them when they told me one day my Easter chick just "went away"? At that age I hadn't been formally introduced to death, but I was somehow aware that at some time things ceased to exist. Trudy sensed it, too. She knew her pony was in trouble, and she would not settle for a lie.

Running into the stall, she kneeled in the straw beside Misty, stroking his forehead and smoothing the scraggly, bushy mane. "What's the matter, Mithty? Don't you feel good?" The pony nickered, his flank vibrating under the strain.

Leah went into the stall after her but didn't try to take her from her pony's side. She knelt down in the straw. "Misty got worse, Trudy. He really doesn't feel very good now. And he's very tired."

Tears welled up in Trudy's eyes as she pleaded with her mother. "But can't Dr. Belly fix him?" Her face contorted. "Fix him up, Mommy, please."

I bent down in the straw next to Trudy and Leah and stroked Misty on the neck. "Dr. Balliet and I are going to do everything we know to help Misty, Trudy. If anyone can help him, Dr. Balliet can."

The little girl rubbed her eyes on the sleeve of her nightie. "God won't take my good pony away, will He, Mommy?"

Leah avoided the question. She beckoned her daughter to come along and reached out a trembling hand, "Come on, let Dr. Balliet give him his medicine. Besides, Misty needs some sleep; you're keeping him up. Tomorrow morning we'll get right up and check on him."

But Trudy had not forgotten her question. She understood her mother's silence, "He won't take him away, will He, Mommy?"

Leah bent over and picked her up, carrying her quietly out of the stall and barn and into the house. We heard a low, muffled crying until the door to the house snapped shut.

Edgar was rummaging about in the back of the truck.

"What are you going to do now?" I asked.

"Everything," he said, his arms lost in bottles of medicine. "I just took a tap from his abdomen." He raised the test tube, the yellow fluid outlined against the truck's light.

"Hey, it doesn't look bad, does it?" I observed.

"Not so far, anyway—but I've got to give it another ten minutes to settle." He pulled a long tube from a side drawer and placed it, together with a pump and jug of mineral oil, inside a metal bucket. "If the tap is bad, then there is nothing I can do for the poor guy—it means he's already ruptured his gut. But if it's all right, then we'll treat for a blockage and hope he'll eventually pass it." He picked out a bottle of injectable laxative, then hooked up an IV system.

"Here, hold out your hands," he said, wrapping two rubber tubes around my arms and piling two IV bottles and a catheter into my hands. "Go ahead; I'm coming right behind you."

The barn's light glowed a bare stinging swath into the night. It was a harsh, eye-smarting brilliance that dared us approach the reality inside. We knew Misty lay precariously close to that "dreamless sleep" beneath that merciless light. I didn't want to go back in. I could have walked more bravely into the dark surrounding woods, through an unknown maze of trees and vines than into this starkly lit barn.

Summoning all my courage, I parted the bright yellow curtain of light and entered the stable, placing an armful of medicines, tubes and syringes on the floor beside Misty's stall. He was standing now; the painkiller was finally beginning to work.

I let him in on a secret before Edgar came back. "Misty, you're going to be fine if Dr. Balliet has anything to say about it because he's the best veterinarian in these parts." Misty turned a fuzzy head and nickered.

For another hour Edgar worked on the pony, setting up the IV line to drip saline solution into his veins throughout the night. Edgar gave him a large dose of mineral oil and an enema, "to get things moving again," as he always says.

A while later Misty's condition was still grave, but at least Edgar offered every chance for recovery. It would have been so easy to have declared the pony incurable and administered the euthanasia solution, thus protecting Leah and us from any more psychological hurt. But Edgar never gives in to the Shadow without a fight. Only the morning would tell if the pony would live.

Leah came out of the house just as we were about to leave. She seemed resigned to Misty's fate. "Thank you for coming out again tonight. We really appreciate it. Is Misty any better?"

"A bit, but his condition is still very serious. The tap came out negative, so we know he's not ruptured; I just hope he didn't take such a setback that we can't pull him around." Edgar started the truck's engine. "Please check every hour or so to see if the catheter is still in the vein; I don't want his neck blowing up with fluid."

"How's Trudy?" I asked.

"Upset. God, I hope that pony doesn't die. It took an hour until she fell asleep. I told her I'd wake her when he got better."

"I'll stop here first thing in the morning to check him. If he should get worse in the next few hours, call me."

The harsh barn light chased us down the stony lane toward home. We stared straight ahead into the blackness encasing us like a tomb, but I couldn't shake the image of the pony struggling to live.

That night sleep came uneasily. We had three hours of undisturbed sleep, yet it was a restless, gnawing kind of sleep. By 7:30 in the morning we were once more driving up the Sigley's stony driveway. The lights had grown softer now, mingled with the dawn. A frosty mist rolled over our truck as we pulled up to the barn. We hurried down the dusty aisle to Misty's stall.

Our eyes adjusted to the dim light within, as daybreak began to leak into the stable from Misty's window. I couldn't believe it: miraculously Misty was standing in a corner of his stall munching hay. He turned to look at us, questioning our intrusion so early this fine day. His IV fluids were still running, his neck swathed in adhesive tape to secure the catheter, and he was still tied to the front of the stall. But, incredibly, he was alive.

"He made it!" I shouted, unable to contain myself. I hopped up and down outside his stall. "Good job, Misty!" I grabbed Edgar, who was right behind me, "You, too, Edgar. Good job!" I squeezed his hand. He laughed, noting the surprised expression on Misty's face. He was obviously pleased with himself.

"Wow, a miracle! I didn't know if I would be able to pull him through," Edgar said, shaking his head.

Then I saw movement in a far corner of Misty's stall. "My God! It's Trudy!" I said, and at that moment Leah, housecoat wrapped tightly around her, walked into the barn.

"Yes, she's been here since just after you left last night. I thought I had put her to sleep, but when I went to bed, she must've sneaked out of the house. I came back to check Misty an hour later and found her fast asleep in a corner of his stall."

The mother admired her child through the stall bars. "So I woke her up and started to take her back to the house, but she begged and carried on so much that I let her stay.

"I dressed her in her cowgirl outfit, wrapped a blanket around her and tucked her into the straw bed here by Misty. Of course, I've not slept a wink all night; I've been out here with Trudy and Misty."

Trudy raised her head from the straw, bits of it sticking in her golden curls.

"Now what did you want to tell Dr. Balliet when he came back this morning?" Leah reminded the little girl.

Trudy's eyes blinked with sleep, and she raised herself on her elbows, "Thank you for saving Mithty, Dr. Belly. Thank you for saving my pony." She giggled shyly and flopped back onto the straw, tucking the blanket up underneath her chin and wriggling down lower into the soft bed.

"I'm just glad to see he's all right." Edgar stepped into the stall and untaped the pony's neck, removing the catheter from the vein. The pony didn't budge an inch, but all the while the slow eyes assessed Edgar, following his arm as he pressed the base of the stethoscope on the flank.

Edgar rested a hand on the pony's back, as Leah and I watched from outside the stall door. He smiled, "Misty, you'll be all right now." Then Edgar faced us. "His gut sounds are good. This guy will be with us for awhile yet, Leah. Now don't give him any grain for the next twenty-four hours, but hay is okay. He's getting his appetite back, I see."

Misty turned to his hay rack and snatched a mouthful of timothy from between the bars. His furry jaw hitched and chomped the good grass, and his expression, unlike that of last night, spelled contentment and comfort.

"Well, can't do anymore here now that everybody's healthy." Edgar grinned. "Ready, Gay? Got to check on a cow with an R.P. at Topman's."

That picture has become indelibly fixed in my memory: Misty standing in his stall, shifting his weight, and munching the good hay, and his little "pardner" sleeping protectively on the straw bed beside him.

from TOUCHED BY ALL CREATURES

Hey! White Kitty!

DIANE M. CIARLONI

I like art and I also like "art." Yes, there is a difference.

Art usually hangs in museums and galleries or, at the very least, in the vestibules of homes owned by people featured on that "Rich and Famous" television program. It goes without saying that this form of art is expensive, and affording an original is possible for only the very, very wealthy.

"Art," on the other hand, can be purchased just about anywhere, including flea markets, garage sales and discount stores. It may cost as little as $5, depending on whether or not it's your lucky weekend. It may or may not be embraced by a nice frame or, really, there's no rule saying it must be a painting, print or litho. It could be a carving or a weaving or a piece of pottery but, on the other hand, it's usually the paintings, prints and lithos that exude a nearly palpable feeling of intense appeal.

Appeal. Therein rests a universal truth. That is, it doesn't matter if a person is viewing art or "art." What matters is whether or not the piece calls out with a pull that's as strong as sucking quicksand. And that is precisely what drew me to the print of the white cat. There seemed to be an invisible but incredibly strong cord curling from the print and wrapping itself around my wrist. There was no way to resist its tug.

It was a large piece, measuring 30 by 36 inches. The frame was solid wood, a bit lighter in color than I preferred, but nice. It also featured a single mat. All those elements were definite positives, but it was the cat that was magnetic enough to literally and physically stop me as I walked (or tried to walk) past.

The cat was white . . . totally. There were no markings. His face and head looked as if they'd begun life as triangular in shape. There were points everywhere. At the top of the triangle were the keen, sharply pointed ears, one on each side of the triangle. The yellow/green eyes were set somewhat inward from the ears.

Follow the triangle downward and it ended in the mouth and chin, forming the third point. The small, flesh-colored nose was the accent point. It made a tiny triangle inside the larger one. Now, maybe due to age, both the left and right sides of the triangle had become somewhat fleshed out, transforming the hard-edged geometric into a softer heart contour.

The white hair was silky, smooth, worn close to the cat's head and body. It was as if a white skullcap covered his entire frame. His face and head were completely visible to the viewer, but the remainder of his body was reminiscent of a jigsaw puzzle, with bits and pieces of it obliterated by leaves and tree branches and the gracefully bending stems of irises and tulips.

He was like an unfinished mosaic. Or maybe a letter without a signature. From one angle he seemed to need someone or something to make him whole. Then, from another angle, he seemed totally self-contained. It was this air of an unsolved mystery that created the white cat's fundamental intrigue. It was also what told me I absolutely must own this piece of ten-dollar "art."

The white cat went home with me, and I hung him on a

generous expanse of wall where I have the luxury of studying him several times each day. Nearly a year passed. The white cat never moved and his gaze never wavered but, still, that sense of incompleteness nagged at me frequently.

One morning I walked outside through my office door. It was early and there was a slight mist hanging from the trees in the woods. The previous fall I'd planted iris and daffodil bulbs in one of the shallow openings, doing what the gardening magazines referred to as "naturalizing" the woods. Whatever the proper terminology, the flowers were just beginning to open. The frilly petals of the irises were deep purple, tipped in lilac. The dark, rich color offered a sense of stability next to the almost reckless abandon of the bright yellow daffodils with their equally bright orange centers.

The woods were always peaceful, and staring into them was like soul-watching. There was a lulling, hypnotic effect combined with a sense of wonder over all the creatures that must be living within the walls of trees and vines. Just then I heard a rustle. Something moved among the leaves. I saw a tiny, fragile branch vibrate ever so gently. What was it?

I could hear the rustle move, move, move, and then stop. From the sounds, it should be almost directly in front of me. I turned slowly, not wanting to frighten it. Had I been looking into a mirror, I'm certain I would have been confronted by an expression of sheer incredulity. There I stood, looking directly into the eyes of the white cat who was captured in the print. Everything was exactly the same. The position and pose were the same. He was half-sitting and half-reclining, with his face and head turned outward. The leaves and branches and the stems of irises and daffodils blocked out chunks of his body. He, just like his lifeless counterpart, appeared to be a work in progress. What was done was lovely, but the missing pieces were needed to fill in the gaps.

"How in the world did this happen?" I wondered aloud.

I didn't attempt to go any closer to the white cat but I did change my angle slightly. When I did, a wave of sadness washed over me. Unlike the white cat in the print, this one was skin and bones. I had no idea how any creature could still be alive in that condition. His face was the same triangular shape as the one in the house, without the filling out that gently kneaded the soft heart contours. Even from a distance, I could see the ugly knobs down his backbone. I knew exactly how they would feel under my fingers. I'd seen them on enough animals. His hip bones were sharply pointed, rising above the profile of his back. The feeling of sadness was still there, but it was shot through with anger . . . the same anger I feel every time someone directly or indirectly abuses an animal.

The cat hadn't moved. I was still watching him and the feeling that pricked along my spine was eerie. I'd seen movies in which a person in a painting suddenly comes alive. Of course, I never believed such a thing could happen but, if not, how did the white cat from the print make his way into the woods? Even the irises were the same!

I squatted down and tried calling, softly.

"Here, white kitty. Come, white cat." He didn't move.

I went into the garage, fixed a bowl of dry food, and set it outside in a spot that I thought he might visit. That was all I could do.

The next morning, when I went into the garage to feed the two outside kitties and to unlock their pet door, I heard a scurrying and then saw a white streak shoot through the small opening. "So," I thought, "he found his way into the garage.

That's good." Everyone must have respected one another's territory since I'd heard no sounds of scuffling during the night.

The white cat continued making frequent visits to the garage, scarfing up whatever food the others might have left. Of course, I always made sure I put out far more than enough for everyone.

The white cat has changed dramatically. Most of the angles are gone and the face has assumed a pronounced heart shape. He still sits behind the leaves and branches and iris stems, with parts of his body seemingly locked forever from view. He doesn't come to me, even though it's been more than eight months. This is something that has never happened in the past. Virtually nothing has altered about him. There is, however, something which seems to have changed about the white cat in the print. Now, when I look at him, I'm no longer struck by that sense of incompleteness. His face, his eyes, are more at peace with the world. It may sound ridiculous, but he seems almost "happy." As if he feels whole.

The white cat in the woods may never respond to me. He may never walk toward my outstretched hand. I may never hear him purr, and I may never feel my own skin come in contact with the glass-like smoothness of his hair.

I don't know what the tie is between the cat in the print and the cat in the woods. I know there is one, but it really doesn't matter because now I know the definition of art is not determined by a price tag. I've also learned the difference between the real and the unreal can be a very, very thin line. And, finally, I've learned there are times when it's far easier to touch and embrace a fantasy than it is to lay even the tip of one finger on the reality.

A Message From the Birds

NANCY B. GIBBS

"How dare those birds sing!" I thought, as I left the nursing home early one Sunday morning. Dozens of birds were chirping in delight, as the sun peeked over the horizon. After a long four years and a very heart-wrenching week, my father had left this world behind and entered a place called heaven. My heart was heavy. I had cried so much that there were no tears left. Silently, my husband and I got into the car and drove away from the nursing home for the last time.

In a few minutes, I picked up my cellular phone, to call my twin sons. Brad picked up the telephone on the first ring. "Did Pot die?" he hesitantly asked.

"Yes, son. He did," I replied.

"Was it about thirty minutes ago?" he asked. I looked at my watch and realized that it was.

We drove to a friend's house where both of my sons were staying. While reminiscing about the love my father shared with his family, Brad told me that he knew exactly when Pot left this world.

"I woke up and thought I heard a little boy's laughter. At first it frightened me, but then I heard a bird on the windowsill. I assumed that it was the bird I had heard. But when the phone rang, I knew that the bird had come to tell me that Pot had died."

Since we hadn't had much sleep that entire week, my husband and I decided to go home to rest. The seventy-mile trip home was long and difficult to make. Before we arrived home, the clouds blackened and a gentle rain fell upon us.

Later that day we returned to my mother's house. My nephew, Clint, asked me exactly what time Pot had passed away. When I told him, he casually mentioned that he awoke about that time and saw a bird sitting outside his window, singing a cheerful song.

Daddy was a bird-lover indeed. After he retired he built dozens of birdhouses. Some were painted red, white and blue, adorning stars and stripes. Others were painted in camouflaged colors. Each one was unique. A birdhouse adorned almost every tree in his yard. He also hung one upon a tree that stood beside the cemetery plot which he had bought in advance. He wanted to take care of as many arrangements as possible before he got sick. The welfare of birds was very important to him.

When we arrived home, I wrote to some of my online friends. For two years they had prayed for Daddy, so I felt that they needed to know about his death. The morning of his funeral, I received an online sympathy card from one of my friends. It was a poem about death. One of the lines stated that when someone dies, a bird gives the message back to the world and sings a silent prayer that makes the rain cry. The words of peace that followed that line gave me a sense of comfort.

I am convinced that God sent all those birds to bring the message to us that Daddy is safe and sound in His arms in heaven. The fact that the rain cried after the announcement was made, reaffirmed my feelings.

A couple of days after Daddy's burial, I went to the cemetery. The wind chimes hanging from the bottom of the birdhouse were making a beautiful sound as the cool breeze gently blew. Down deep in my heart, I felt Daddy's presence.

I have the assurance that one day I'll see my daddy again on the streets of gold. I also believe there will be thousands of birdhouses, hanging on every tree in heaven and that Daddy will have built them all with his own perfect hands.

A Promise on Paws

LEIGH SINGH

When I was a little girl, my grandfather used to tell me that every part of life held the promise of something good. My Pop Pop said if I believed in that promise hard enough, sooner or later I would find a good thing—even in life's most difficult situations. Sometimes it was easy to believe what my grandfather told me, especially when the two of us spent time together on his farm. The deep, dulcet greeting of a gentle milking cow, the fragrance of freshly-turned earth in the garden, and the soft unspoiled sweetness of a newborn kitten taught me the truth in my grandfather's words. I held tightly to such beautiful reminders. Still, as a child born with cerebral palsy, I thought I had found something my Pop Pop had gotten wrong. Pop Pop said that every part of life held the promise of something good. His words made sense for things like freshly-plowed gardens and newborn kittens; but they didn't make sense for cerebral palsy. I couldn't find anything good in living with my disability.

Cerebral palsy was a harsh and unrelenting part of young life. My days were measured by physical pain, difficult therapy, frightening operations, and the realization that no matter how hard I tried, there were some things that I just could not do. I used to watch my childhood friends walk smoothly across a room, but when I tried to do the same, my muscles refused to cooperate. My body behaved like some intricate toy that never worked the way I wanted it to. I underwent my first operation when I was two. By the time I was ten years old, I had endured more surgical procedures than most people face in a lifetime. The bones in my ankles were reconstructed, the muscles in my legs were lengthened, even my eyes were repositioned. Every operation promised to improve my physical body. I tried to remember that even the most painful procedures could make things better, but remembering that was hard.

Cerebral palsy made a lot of things hard; and it wasn't the kind of condition that eventually faded away. It did not fade away with therapy, or braces, or prayers hung on every star in the heavens. My CP did not fade away even after a dozen operations. I made my way through childhood with a patchwork of surgical scars on my body, a closet full of braces, and a whole sky full of prayers; but walking was still a formidable task. It demanded determination, concentration, and good luck. If I had all three of these, I could usually move across a room without crashing into anything. For me, that was graceful. Far too often, my poise would forsake me in mid-stride and I would tumble to the ground like some weary, wind-tossed sparrow.

With time, practice, and patience, I discovered ways to manage many of the physical challenges of my disability. Still, the most daunting struggle I faced could not be reckoned with in an operating room or on a physical therapy mat. CP had an insidious hold on my heart. I did my best to act happy and secure, but beneath my eager smile, I felt guilty and afraid. For years, even saying the words *cerebral palsy* made me redden with shame. I thought that my own worth was measured not by the way I lived, but by the way I walked. I was afraid that other people would see my disabled body and somehow decide there wasn't enough to love in the person they saw. That fear surrounded me like an immense stone wall. I could not open up to the people around me. I could not believe in the person I was created to be. I could only hide behind that wall.

Since my grandfather had told me that every part of life held the promise of something good, I tried to believe in that promise. In the silent harbor of my heart, I prayed that God would reveal whatever goodness could come out of my disability. Still, even after years of trying, I could not find anything good in having to live every moment of my life with cerebral palsy. Then, when I was twenty-three years old, something good found me. That good thing was a service dog named Slugger.

In the early spring of 1991, Slugger was a lively handful of sunshine-colored fluff. Pure Labrador joy bubbled up inside him and escaped in a steady stream of happy puppy wiggles. As soon as Sylvia Fisher, the president of Caring Canine Companions, saw Slugger, she knew he was destined to make a difference. Sylvia enlisted the help of Vickie Polk and other CCC volunteers who trained assistance dogs for physically disabled individuals. Thanks to their skill and dedication, the precocious, bright-eyed puppy was transformed into a certified mobility assistance dog.

I will always remember that wondrous March morning when I met Slugger for the first time. I remember how his tail waved in an easy, joyful hello, how his brown eyes sparkled with friendly curiosity. I was smitten in a matter of moments. Slugger was the most incredible animal I could have imagined; and I soon discovered there was more to this dog than I had guessed, *much* more. As a certified service dog, Slugger had mastered basic obedience skills. He knew how to retrieve dropped items, open doors, and bark on command. This extraordinary dog had even learned how to provide support while navigating steps and hills with his handler.

It had taken nearly two years for Slugger to learn the skills that defined his role as a service dog. It took the two of us several months to find the easy cadence of our own working rhythm. With patience and training, Slugger and I began building the special bond that joins an assistance dog and a human partner. We graduated as a team in the summer of 1993. Although we still had plenty to learn from each other, I knew then that Slugger would make a difference in my life. At the time, I had no idea *how* great a difference that would be.

My partnership with Slugger brought a new kind of freedom to my life. When the two of us began our career as a service dog team, I was attending graduate school. With Slugger by my side, basic tasks like carrying heavy text books and walking across a crowded campus became easier than I had ever hoped they would be. I no longer had to rely on other people to give me a hand when I was going up a hill. If I dropped a pencil during one of my classes, Slugger would quickly retrieve it for me. Many times, my faithful canine companion even kept me from falling. The familiar perils of rugged sidewalks, slippery floors, and ice-covered steps no longer held me captive.

My service dog brought me the gift of physical freedom; yet even more precious than that freedom was the gift he brought to my heart. Slugger touched my heart with an extraordinary and unconditional love. His was a love that kept pace when I danced and held steadfast when I stumbled. In sweet, unspoken ways, that love eased the pain in my heart. It helped me find the strength to conquer the fears that had held me hostage for so long. My service dog's unwavering devotion taught me how to believe in the person I was created to be.

With Slugger by my side, I learned to define myself not by what I had to overcome but by what I had the courage to become.

My service dog and I have lived and worked together for almost seven years now; and in his gentle way, Slugger continues to share certain Labrador lessons with me. These lessons have made me a much wiser person. Thanks to my dog, I have discovered that white fur on a dark skirt can make a wonderful fashion statement. I have learned that every good partnership is a matter of give and take. I have also discovered that sometimes God puts life-changing blessings on paws. And now, at last, I understand what my grandfather meant when he said that every part of life holds the promise of something good. Thanks to Slugger, I know he was right.

Snowy

ALICE C. BATEMAN

My life has been filled with four-legged friends. My earliest memories and every single photograph of me as a child feature pets. My family lived on a farm where we had almost every kind of animal at one time or another.

One memorable spring, my dad brought home a whole big box of fluffy yellow chicks, which I immediately fell in love with. I can still hear the chirp-chirp of those little chicks through the days and nights that we kept them in the house. The spring must have suddenly turned cold that year, so the babies had to stay in the house for a few days. It didn't take my tender young heart long to learn that some things on the farm were not meant to be pets, as the beautiful fluffy babies rapidly turned into chickens, and then dinner. After their initial fluffiness, chickens did not seem to make good companions anyway, and I was never close to them after they'd grown.

Some of the animals on the farm became not pets, but friends. When I was very young, we had one cow by the name of Daisy. She was not a pet, and no one else in the family seemed to care much for her, but to me she was a friend. In my mind I would talk to her, and fancy that she answered.

At six, I was shipped off to school in the big yellow bus, taking me away from all my four-legged friends at home every day. But each day as we'd drive past Daisy in her field, I'd send her a message and she'd send one back. Just simple things like "Hello" and "How are you?" or any little secrets I had, and she'd gaze at me with her big, soft brown eyes, and I knew she'd understood. She always turned to watch the bus going in the morning and coming back in the afternoon; she was my landmark to tell me I was home, my confidante.

One day, without warning, I came home on the bus and Daisy wasn't in her field. It wasn't until suppertime that I got a chance to ask why she wasn't there, and where she was. Someone at the table—I don't remember who (I have five brothers and five sisters)—said, "You're eating her."

I choked on my food and began to cry. No one had ever told me that Daisy was food. To me, it was like being told I was eating my best friend. From that point forward, I could not eat meat—I would have the tiniest portion they would allow, and have great difficulty swallowing that down. As an adult, I became a vegetarian, and haven't eaten any flesh of any kind for twenty years now.

The only being on the farm who could console me at that time was my cat, Snowy, a white cat with blue eyes and fluffy fur. She had the bluest eyes I'd ever seen, and seemed to be able to look right inside me and feel how badly I felt. I remember burying my face in her fur and crying my heart out for my friend Daisy. Snowy was the only one who seemed to understand that my little heart was broken and grieving for a dead friend.

Snowy shadowed me for days; if she wasn't in my arms, she was at my heels. I remember going back into the forest by myself the next day, to get away from the rest of them. I now considered them all heartless for eating Daisy. I felt as if all light had gone out of my world. And if they could eat Daisy, would I be next? I had a very active and maybe unusual imagination as a small child, and that didn't seem outside the realm of possibility to me. It was almost as if I knew the animals as people, not as beasts; that there was a psychic connection between their souls and mine.

Snowy came and found me in the trees, rubbed all around my hunched-over little body, purring as loudly as she could, as if to say, "Don't cry, you still have other friends here."

Of course, I was afraid that by that night, Snowy or any or all of my other animal friends might end up on the supper table. Nobody took the trouble to explain to me that some animals are raised for food, and others for pets. That was in the days when children were "seen and not heard," so we didn't have the freedom to ask questions and get satisfactory answers.

My cat Snowy, after slowly circling me to offer what comfort she could, nudged her head in between my arms, which were propped on my knees. My hands covered my face, and tears leaked out between my fingers. She nudged gently until I took my hands away from my face and held them out to her, inviting her onto my lap.

I'll never forget the look of kindness and compassion in that cat's blue eyes as she gazed into mine. I could hear her in my mind, telling me that everything would be okay, and that I didn't have to worry about them eating her or the other cats or dogs, that they were safe from the forks and appetites of the family.

I don't think my tender and loving young psyche would have survived that experience as well as it did without the ministrations of Snowy, a loving and compassionate being wrapped in a small creature of fur and claws.

Millie

THIRZA PEEVEY

$\mathcal{M}$illie had a rough start in life. A young woman stopping for gas between Chicago and Lexington noticed some rough-looking characters in the corner of the gas station selling Beagle puppies out of the back of their pickup. After filling her tank, she went over to admire the puppies and play with them for a moment. They were all beautiful soft eyes and long ears that they constantly stepped on, falling over themselves as they played. The young woman would have loved to have one, but her apartment management didn't allow pets. Sadly, she started to turn away.

As she left, one of the men called to her and said they were planning to kill the runt because they couldn't sell her. She could have the puppy if she wanted it. She drew her five-foot frame up to its full size, told the men what she thought of them and took the tiny puppy.

She worried the rest of the way home, wondering what she and her husband would do with the puppy. She needn't have worried. Her husband worked for the man who would be-come my husband, and my husband has a weakness for dogs.

The next morning, when Gary produced that tiny puppy from his coat pocket, Tom was smitten. He wasn't sure about taking her, though, as it was the height of the breeding season on the bluegrass thoroughbred horse farm where he worked. Breeding season, for a brood mare manager, means getting up at 4:30 to tease all the mares by 6:00 when the reproductive vet arrives. After the vet checks the mares that the teaser showed interest in, the manager has to schedule covers for them and van them to the farms where their particular stallions were kept. Around that, he has to supervise the crews who are cleaning stalls, feeding, caring for the foals, etc. Then all night he delivers new babies. Tom just didn't see how he could fit a puppy into that schedule.

Then Gary put the puppy in his hand. The puppy immediately launched herself into the huge apple fritter Tom had in his other hand. She ate the monstrous thing in three bites. Then she rolled over, displaying a belly that was now wider than long, and smiled. Tom was hooked. When he stopped laughing, he agreed to take her.

Because she wasn't housebroken yet, Tom carried her with him and his other old dog in the truck all day. That way he could keep an eye on her. Everyone on the farm became quite enamored of her. Having had such a rough start, Millie seemed determined to devote her life to bringing joy and laughter into the world. She did everything with gusto, then turned around to face you and collect her payment of laughter. When I joined the staff, Millie decided that it was her personal responsibility to help me get fit and make it fun to do so. Everywhere I went, if I carried a lead shank, she would grab it and wrestle it for all she was worth.

One particular coworker, Jim, was even fonder of Millie than the rest of the crew, and he worried about something happening to her. Tom would often leave her at the barn with us. When he did, Millie would play tricks on Jim to tease him.

Her favorite was to run into the culvert that lay under the farm road in front of the barn. When she didn't come out, Jim would get concerned and get on his knees by the culvert, stick his head inside and call her. When he did, she would run out the other end, cut back across the road and hide behind Jim, wagging her tail. When he gave up and got up, he would find her behind him, grinning, wagging, woofing and dancing. ✓

One morning, I brought home-baked cookies for the staff. When we got a break, Jim sat in the chair in the office, put his feet on the desk and picked up a cookie. Just as it touched his lips, Millie leaped into his lap, stole the cookie and ran to the far corner of the office where she ate it. Jim looked at his empty fingers, then at Millie, then at the empty fingers, turned to Millie and drawled, "By Gawd, Millie, you won't do that again." Millie sat up, wagged her tail and barked in answer. Jim reached for another cookie. Just as it touched his lips, she did it again.

A short time later, Tom left the farm. While he was looking for a new job, Jim and I baby-sat the dogs for him each day. I began taking Millie and Tom's other dog, Lady, to lunch with me. At a local fast-food place, I would get a burger for myself and a junior burger to split between them. Naturally, this was the highlight of their day.

One day, the girl in the fast food drive-through crooned to Millie, "Oh, aren't you cute!"

Millie sat up and barked, as if to say, "You're not so bad yourself."

The girl looked back over her shoulder and called to her coworkers, "Look at this Beagle. She's so cute!"

That was all the invitation Millie needed. She figured she would save them the trip and go to them. Springing across my lap, she leaped through the open window. The only thing that stopped her from having a romp through the restaurant kitchen at lunch hour was my reflexes. I just managed to catch a hind leg as she leaped across me and I pulled her back.

Millie's life's work became serious around the time Tom left the farm. During his last few weeks on the farm, one of his friends became seriously ill with Guillaume Barre's syndrome and was bedridden. Since Tom wasn't working, he went several times a week to take care of Kathy's shopping, housework and yard work. Millie didn't always want to stay with me. She seemed to feel a duty to go along and comfort Kathy. One day when Tom dropped Millie off at the barn, he left his window open a split second too long. Millie ran alongside the car as he drove away and, with perfect timing, leaped through the open window of the moving car to land squarely in Tom's lap. From then on, Millie went along and entertained Kathy with her frantic skittering around the house on hardwood floors. When she tired, she would leap into bed with Kathy, roll on her back and give her patented Beagle grin. There they would sleep together all afternoon. Kathy said the warmth and contact was comforting and aided her recovery. To this day she refers to it as Beagletherapy. And so do we.

The first time I took Tom home to meet my folks, my stepfather didn't particularly want the dogs in the house. I didn't want Tom to know that the dogs weren't welcome, so I brokered a deal that the dogs could stay in the back bedroom while we ate dinner. They were used to being house dogs and it wasn't fair to leave them locked at home for eight to ten hours while Tom drove 100 miles each way. It wasn't any better to leave them out in the car in the cold at Christmastime.

Millie sang the whole time. When Tom let her out of the

bedroom after dinner, she leaped the couch, front to back and end to end in one six-foot-long, four-foot-high jump that never touched the couch. "You don't want me jumping on the furniture," she seemed to say. "Okay, I won't touch it. But, that won't keep me from jumping over it."

At the next place Tom worked, the owner had an eighteen-month-old daughter. Millie sneaked up on the child as she was sitting in a car seat on the ground outside the barn. Millie grabbed the child's Raggedy Ann doll from her hands and bounded off with it, throwing the doll in the air and racing in circles. The child's wail pierced the air. "Raggedy Ann, Raggedy Ann," she shrieked. Millie didn't know what to make of this. She was used to getting laughter for her antics. She never meant to make anyone cry. She screeched to a halt, and dropped Raggedy Ann, looking utterly perplexed. Fortunately, Millie managed to make amends for that slip. In fact, that family loves her so much that they baby-sit for her and our new puppy whenever we go away. They can't bear to think of her in a kennel. In fact, she is the only dog in the house that is allowed on the furniture and sleeps in bed with the little girl when she stays. If they can't keep her, other current and former employees who remember Millie vie for the chance to keep her.

Millie next took her Beagletherapy on the road. The year we married, Tom took a job working for Central Kentucky Riding for the Handicapped, a program that puts adults and children with disabilities on horseback. Millie went along. She had started her life going to work with Tom every day, and by now had perfect work manners. At the program, she became the first contact with animals for many kids, and eased the transition to horseback for many a frightened child.

One child came to visit the program before classes started.

All of four years old, the little girl was terrified by even the oldest, gentlest, smallest pony in the barn. Millie was perturbed by her hysterical crying and went to comfort her. Plunking herself in front of the child, she whined and licked the girl's face. Soon the little girl was petting Millie and calling her a "good doggie." Eventually, her crying quieted and she became calm enough to pet the pony. When classes started, she was brave enough to ride with the class.

Now in her later years, Millie is a contented shop dog. Life on farms got to be too much for Tom and me, now that we are old married fogies. I became a teacher, and Tom works in a saddle shop. Millie still goes to work every day and moves from sunny spot to sunny spot throughout the day like a cat. When it's cloudy, she sleeps in the pile of horse blankets on the showroom floor. She faithfully gets up to greet and cheer every customer who comes through the door. You see, she feels it is her job. She has spent her life brightening people's lives, and even though she is a bit gray now, she isn't about to stop doing what she does best. Retirement is the furthest thing from her mind.

I Named Her Molly

BERTHA M. SUTLIFF

felt as if I was becoming a prisoner in my own home. My days were so lonely. My husband Robert would leave for work at 5 a.m., making sure I was comfortable and had access to my needs. He didn't return until a little past 2 in the afternoon. He would call a couple of times to ask how I was doing, but other than that, my window next to my chair and the TV were my access to the outside world.

I heard the truck pull into the garage and the door slam. I sat there anxiously awaiting his voice to tell me he was home. After a few minutes I began to wonder where he was or what he was doing. Suddenly, I heard the front door open and his wonderful, "I'm home."

He walked into the kitchen and set his lunch bucket on the cabinet. I could see him through the doorway of the living room where I sat. "What is that you have?" I asked.

"What?" he replied.

"What is that?" I was staring at the dark little bundle in his hand.

"Oh, you mean this," and he held out a small kitten toward me.

"Oh, Robert, where did you find that?" I reached out and took the tiny bundle of dark fur.

"Mama had it. Someone dropped it in the park and some-how it managed to crawl into her yard. She's been feeding it with a bottle, but now it's eating from a bowl. She said it keeps getting out of its box and she's afraid she's going to step on it. I asked her if I could take it. I don't want her to trip and fall try-ing to avoid it." Robert's mother was elderly and lived alone next door to us. She loved cats, but because of her age she was a little unsteady on her feet.

"You asked her for this cat?"

"Yeah, I asked her for the cat," he replied.

"Robert, how many times have I asked you if I could have a cat, and you always said no?"

"I know, I know, maybe she'll be company to you."

I reached my arms up to his face and gently kissed him. "Thank you."

I had inherited a dreaded disease from my parents. As a young-ster I was strong and a hard worker. Raised on a farm, I had worked in the fields beside my dad and done my share of the farm work. After I married, we lived on a piece of land my dad had given me and I made it into a small homestead. My two sons and I built fences and made chicken coops. We walked the mountains and ridges together to find the best wild fruits and the best fishing holes. Now, as I'm getting close to middle age, things are slowing down. My sons are grown and have families of their own.

We gave up our country home and moved to town to care for Robert's mother next door. I put a private day care in my home to help with expenses. After six years of satisfied bliss, caring for the children of my friends, I began to feel the ache in my back and legs. At night it became harder and harder for me to find the right spot in the bed where I could be comfortable. Then the day came when I bent down to pick up a beautiful baby girl and I went to my knees. My back grabbed, taking my breath with it. I managed to crawl to the couch. Calling all the children to me, I sat there the rest of the afternoon telling them stories and waiting for their parents to pick them up. The next day I went to see my doctor.

He was just a medical doctor but he knew when he saw the x rays that something was wrong. My back was in sad shape. I was going to have to quit my business. That was when I resigned myself to the recliner in the living room by the window and the TV. I knew the inevitable was yet to come.

I named the kitten Molly. She looked like a Molly to me. She was constantly by my side. We played, we slept and we watched the birds outside the window. I think she even watched the TV with me. She became my confidante, my listener of oh's and ouch's. She would rub my arms and nuzzle my chin when the tears fell. I don't know who was whose pet. Was I hers or was she mine?

Molly grew into a beautiful black short-hair cat with touches of gold scattered in her fur. She loved Robert and me, and we in turn loved her.

When she was around 2 years of age, I had to have surgery on my back. The night before I left for the hospital, I held her and talked to her. I told her I was going away for awhile but I would be back. Molly wanted to lick my feet and hands. It was as if she was saying, "Let me help you get ready." While I was gone, my husband said she would not eat and constantly cried at my window. On my return home, she bounded around the house like a young kitten. I was sedated and secluded in my bedroom with the door closed to her. Time and time again she would go to the bedroom door and cry, scratching and pushing on it trying to gain entrance.

A couple of days later, the home-nursing people brought me a hospital bed and set it up in the front room of our house. At first they tried to keep Molly out of the room and off of my bed. When they came she would run and hide, but as soon as they left she came running back to me. Molly had her place on the bed, right next to me.

In time I was able to get out of the bed and walk with the aid of a walker. Molly walked every step with me. The nurses would try and make her go away, but to no avail. Molly was going to nurse me back to health whether they liked it or not. She would bring me her toys and I would play with her, sitting on our bed. My husband would look at us and shake his head.

Finally the day came when I no longer needed the walker in the bed. I think Molly was just as happy as I was to see it taken down and the nurses leave for the last time.

Today I am doing fine. I have some problems with my legs from nerve damage, and when they hurt, Molly will come and lie across them. I can feel the warmth of her body and the massage of her purr. I look at her at times and I wonder, does God send us a special angel in special forms, like maybe a cat, a cat with black short hair and a sprinkle of gold in her fur?

Nell, a Cat With a Star Complex

CAROL WALLACE

If it weren't for a college play rehearsing in Scranton, Little Nellope would have been left to her almost-certain fate—abandoned with a sibling underneath a tree in the woods. When Rochelle found her, she was alive and her companion was dead. They were only a couple of weeks old.

I never knew if Rochelle was normally the rescuing type, or whether she only picked up the little kitten because her brother needed one as a prop in a play he was in. Which is how Nell came to spend the next few weeks living in a theater.

Tiny kittens are always cute, but Nell came along at a time when I had just lost Buckle, my little best friend of eight years, to leukemia. I was rehearsing a different play (it was to be an evening of one-act plays) but was more than willing to take the tiny thing and hold her when she wasn't needed on stage.

I am glad that the director's wife noticed my attraction to Nell. When the show was over she asked me if I would like to take the little star home—and, of course, I did. She was handed over to me just before I had to teach a class in Media Law—and since I was reluctant to leave her alone in my office, she came to class with me. She spent most of the lecture falling asleep on various notebooks, but no one seemed to mind.

My cousin Donna had a good way of naming cats. She said that you should always call them after something you love. So I named my new kitten Nell, because that was the name of the character I played in my best all-time stage performance. And since Nell was a theater cat, it seemed appropriate.

And that is how I came to have a college-educated cat with a star complex. At least that is how we came to interpret her somewhat stand-offish behavior. She didn't seem to care for laps, and appeared only to tolerate petting.

Nevertheless, a few weeks later my husband brought me a pure black kitten for my birthday, because up until Nell came to live with us, all of our cats had been black. Nell appeared outraged. I expected the initial growls because that seems like one of those rituals cats go through before they settle into peaceful coexistence. But Nell and Peabody never settled into anything peaceful at all. We had to find them separate feeding stations, and tried to make sure that if one was inside, the other was out.

Normally, two sane people might have interpreted this as jealously, but my husband and I had already labeled poor Nell as a feline version of a prima donna.

Then three things made me rethink my position. The first was simply the fact that every morning as my feet hit the floor getting out of the bed, Nell's head would appear as she came out from under it. So I had to admit that she had an affection for us, even if she wasn't very good at showing it.

She would follow me down the steps then, as I groped my way to the coffee pot—and at some point speed up so that she was directly in front of me instead of behind me. This is NOT a good behavior with someone who isn't alive without her quota of caffeine, and so I complained to her every day about how one day she would be the death of me. Soon she decided to retreat to the step behind me, but would catch up to me and stand on the tread that I was on, looking up, one paw slightly raised.

I thought she only wanted a "good cat!" compliment. But I happened to glance behind me as I passed her and saw her quickly start to lick that paw and leg as if that was the only reason it was lifted. But something clicked in my caffeine-deprived brain: Cats do that frantic licking when they are embarrassed. She had wanted me to pet her.

After that I took pains to stop whenever she assumed that "one step up" place—which put her within easy reach for my petting her without having to stoop. I was ashamed of myself for not really paying attention to her, and fobbing her off with a quick label.

But she still was not an affectionate cat. Not for a few more months. Not until she got fleas.

It seems odd to think of a cat being fortunate in having fleas. This was before PreCor allowed you to get rid of fleas with a simple dab on the cat's neck. This was when the cat's people would have to somehow imprison the cat on their lap and comb a flea liquid through its fur until it was saturated.

We did Peabody first and it was a total nightmare of squealing, wriggling cat with unsheathed claws. We got it done, but not easily. And given that as a preview of things to come, the only reason we even tried to tackle Nell was that we were sick of being flea-bitten.

My husband lost the flip and had to assume the role of restrainer. I poured out the flea shampoo and made sure the comb remained moist—and assumed a defense position that would keep Nell from escaping before she was sufficiently soaked.

Neither of us was surprised at Nell's initial struggle, but we were shocked speechless when she suddenly quieted down and sat quite patiently while we combed and combed. Pretty soon we were even more amazed to realize that she was purring.

"It's the attention!" It hit me suddenly that Nell had not been stand-offish at all. There WAS no star complex. In fact, she was merely shy and terrified of rejection. Perhaps it was her early abandonment, or the uncertainty of her early weeks. According to my vet's best estimate, she was about 7 weeks old when I got her, meaning she grew up almost entirely without a mother's love. Forcing her to sit and be stroked, even if it was with flea shampoo, made her feel wanted. I was well and truly ashamed of myself.

Her recovery was not instantaneous, of course. It took several months of picking her up and putting her on our laps, holding on so she couldn't escape and then petting her. We developed a ritual whereby I go down one step in the morning and she pauses on the top landing. I pet her for a few seconds, and then she peaceably trails me down the steps for breakfast.

Sometimes now she appears on my lap without warning—still so silently and unobtrusively that I scarcely realize that she is there. But she has become a companion now, trailing along beside me as I walk through the gardens, sitting on top of the desk and watching me work, sometimes leaping up to the bed to lie beside me in the mornings. She is even learning to accept the fact that she is not an only cat, but that this doesn't mean she isn't loved. It merely means that she is an individual, as all cats are, and that she needs to be recognized that way—just as our two-legged friends do.

And I in turn have learned how important it is to listen to your pets and not rely on preconceived notions about how cats are supposed to act. I'm glad that Nell finally managed to get her message through to us. We are all much happier because she did.

Eureka!

LONNIE HULL DuPONT

Many years ago, I worked in a publishing house on the west coast. A born-and-raised country girl from Michigan, I nevertheless found that I absolutely loved city life, even though it was often lonely for me. I loved the ethnic diversity in my neighborhood, and I even loved the noise of all of us living in that small area. It was like village life. I enjoyed the sidewalks, the parks, the theatres, the coffeehouses. I also was now meeting people with all kinds of different life philosophies. Some of that was interesting to me, some of it was not.

There was a consulting editor who occasionally presented projects to us at the publishing house. His area of expertise and mine rarely dovetailed, and I often personally found his philosophies—and ultimately his projects—so alien that I mentally zoned out or made up grocery lists in my head during his presentations. One day this particular editor was presenting a project, and I had mentally drifted off as usual. Suddenly I heard him say: "We've lost our connection to the earth. We've lost our connection to the animals."

I stopped in my tracks . . . mentally, that is. He was right. At least for me, he was right. A great sadness swept over me. I felt like weeping. I began to see the animals of my lifetime parade before me, and I realized that until a few years before, I'd always had pets—or at least access to lots of animals—and I missed them. And the thing was, I hadn't noticed it until now. No wonder I felt so lonely when it wasn't really my disposition to feel that way: I had no animal friends in my world.

Sitting in the meeting, I remembered the creatures of my childhood—a childhood spent largely without other children. I remembered the cats who slept with me, one of them starting to give birth on my bed one night. The sweet family dog who was terrified of thunderstorms. The wild baby rabbits abandoned by their mother. The dog I trained in German when I was learning that language. Our palomino horse and the brown-eyed ponies. The stray rooster, the goldfish, the guppies, the triplet fawns. Our neighbor's huge, gorgeous draft horses he used for plowing when every other farmer used machinery. And how I used to sing to his cows until they'd line up at the fence to listen.

Now that I traveled a lot for my career and often moved on short notice for it, I purposely had not allowed myself a pet in years. It simply wasn't practical to have one. I suddenly ached inside about that.

We've lost our connection to the earth. We've lost our connection to the animals. What had happened to me?

The sadness stayed with me all day, and eventually I buried it. I went on about my life and my career. I found myself getting to know other people's dogs more and paying attention to the birds outside my apartment, but that was all I allowed myself of the animal world.

Many years later I married, and a few years after that, my husband and I decided to move back near my family home in Michigan. My parents were elderly, and we felt the need to be near them. We bought a big, very old farmhouse in a remote part of the state, and though I missed city life desperately, I felt we'd made the right move.

For many reasons, we had moved lock, stock, and barrel three times in ten months, cross-country, cross-state, before we settled into that farmhouse. All that moving took a toll on both of us. My husband's sweet disposition disappeared for awhile, though it did come back.

As for me, I began feeling anxious all the time. In the pit of my stomach I had vague feelings of dread that never really seemed to go away. For some reason, these feelings especially raised their heads whenever I drove down the road to my new home. There was a big S curve, and until I maneuvered that and could see my house standing in the distance, I felt anxious and worried. If it was at night and that big old farmhouse loomed in the dark, I felt more anxiety, even though I'd never been afraid of a dark, empty house before. But it really wasn't about the house.

Some people might have suggested anti-anxiety medication, and I'm not against that. I'm convinced, however, that these feelings were about my spirit rather than my mental state, and even while I was feeling them, I had an inkling that that was so. I observed my feelings, kept them to myself, and went about my days, hoping relief was in sight.

One of the nicer things about moving near my family was that my relationship with my older sister picked up from where it was fifteen years ago when we'd been very close. We once again could enjoy each other's company. She and her husband had a longhorn steer ranch a few miles away, and I would hang out at her house many an afternoon.

A few months after our moving to the farmhouse, calving time began at the ranch. There were eighteen live births that spring, and my sister checked up often on the longhorn mommies-to-be. One humid spring day when I showed up at my sister's house, she said, "Get back in your car and follow me. One of the heifers is going to give birth today. I won't be able to stay long, but you might want to watch it."

We drove back to a field where the big-bellied heifer staggered back and forth, the front legs of her soon-to-be-born baby slowly inching out of her swaying body. We stayed in our cars with the motors off so that we would not distract her in her labor. Not much more happened for awhile, and eventually my sister slowly drove off as planned. I considered leaving too, but I had nothing pressing to do that afternoon, so I rolled down my window and watched. There was a light shower, and the fragrance of the rain and the wet earth combined with the earthier animal smells felt familiar. I was glad that I could take all those odors; years of pitching horse manure in my youth had made it so.

After awhile, the heifer moved to a shed, but it was open on both ends, allowing me visibility, albeit in silhouette. The heifer lay down for only a few minutes. Then she sprang back up and lowered herself down on her front legs to a kneeling position. She licked and nudged a dark form that didn't move. I was a little concerned about that lack of movement, then was distracted by the most wonderful sight: several longhorn cows with their young calves in tow were moving across the field toward the shed. They apparently had heard something I did not, and they were going at a brisk clip. When they got to the shed, they queued up single file and, one by one, reached their noses down to sniff and nuzzle the newborn.

I'm sure a rancher could tell me why they did this, but to my eyes, they were welcoming the new wee one to the world.

The light rain continued, and the cows and calves sort of hovered around the shed. Eventually the mother nudged the little one's head up. I could see that all was well, and I drove back to my sister's.

After an early supper, I decided to go see if the newborn was on his feet. I drove back to where he'd been born, and sure enough, there he was, standing wobbily, flanked by his mother and a longhorn auntie. He wasn't walking; he was still working on standing on those long young legs. At one point, he sneezed or something and collapsed on the ground. It was awfully cute. Mother and Auntie watched him for a moment, then nosed him back up. Some of the birth cord was still hanging from his belly, and his mother leaned down and snagged it with the end of her horn. He managed to stay upright for that.

I continued to watch them until dusk. At some point, sitting there in the light spring rain with the engine off and my window down, I realized that I had not worried about anything at all in hours. I had been completely absorbed in the longhorns' world. For the first time in many, many months, the pit of my stomach was completely relaxed.

Then in my mind I heard the sentences I hadn't thought about in years, loud and clear: *We've lost our connection to the earth. We've lost our connection to the animals.*

Oh my, I thought. I had. And it appeared that, *eureka,* I'd found those connections again!

Later that same month a stray kitten came to our home. We took her in. The next year another stray kitten came to our house, and we took her in. My husband and I believe that both of these creatures were sent to us for a reason.

Today when I maneuver the S curve, I can hardly wait to see the big old farmhouse, because now it is never empty.

There are always two little warm bodies waiting for me. When I pet the cats and talk to them and watch them interact with each other, I feel grounded and calm.

I have to be with animals. I have to. I'm so grateful that I've found them again.

CHEER UP!

*"...And so it is you cheer me,
My old friend."*

JAMES WHITCOMB RILEY

*Y*ou cannot possibly remain glum when an animal is around. They seem to look at the world through the eyes of hope. Walk down a street after a storm and you'll hear the birds sing as they come out of their shelters and look for food. There are no notes of complaint in their voices, only rejoicing that the clouds are gone and the sun is shining.

The Gift of a Happy Memory

RENIE SZILAK BURGHARDT

There is an old homestead in my neighborhood, with a weathered farmhouse, surrounded by rolling fields dotted with oak and hickory trees, encircled by a forest of more hickory and oak trees, and blessed with a small, winding creek that flows at the bottom of the field. Although the homestead had seen good days, with children thriving in the homey, country environment, it had been sadly neglected in the past few years, especially after the passing of my friend and neighbor, Anne. After Anne died, her husband, Dan, in his sixties, went to live with his son and family in St. Louis, and their trips to the old homestead had gotten scarce. Until Dan's family decided that a family reunion on the Old Home Place would be just the perfect setting for Dan's upcoming birthday, since he had become somewhat depressed over being away from it.

So it was a pleasant surprise to hear that they were planning this reunion, last spring. Dan's two sons, their wives, and two grandchildren all came down one weekend to spruce up the house and fields for the reunion. They put a fresh coat of paint on the house, and bush-hogged the fields, while the grandchildren—ten-year-old Josh, and his ten-year-old cousin,

Lizbeth—happily roamed the fields and woods, just as their grandfather used to do as a boy.

"Things have been tough for Dad since Mom's passing. We feel that his spirit needs a lift. We're hoping that this reunion will help," Dan's daughter-in-law, Debbie, told me when she stopped at my place to invite me to the reunion and birthday party. Since I had been good friends with Dan and Anne, I was honored to be invited.

So, while the adults worked that weekend, Josh and his cousin Lizbeth, roamed the hills and hollows, collected neat-shaped rocks, and talked about what to give their Gramps for his birthday. Josh wanted his gift to be really special. Something that would truly lift his grandfather's spirit. But what would that be? he pondered and pondered.

A few days before the reunion, Josh and his mother drove to the Old Home Place again to finish last-minute preparations. But Josh was feeling desperate by this time, for he still didn't have a gift for Gramps, Debbie said. "I told Josh that we'd run to town in the morning, so he could look in the stores again. He'd better pick something out this time, the reunion is the day after tomorrow. But it seems he wants to give his grandfather something really special, not just any old store-bought thing."

"That's so thoughtful of Josh," I said.

"Yes, except that he's driving me batty. I told him to just draw him a picture or write him a poem, like Lizbeth is doing, but he didn't like that idea one bit."

Well, it seems that Josh was walking through the rolling, rocky field that afternoon when he felt something bumpy under his foot. He leaned down to examine his find since, to him, rocks were the jewels of the farm, and he lugged count-less ones back to the city with him. But he was surprised that

the bump under his foot wasn't a rock at all. No, it was something even better than a rock! Then, picking up his find, he
raced across the field toward the house, whooping so loudly
that countless birds, looking for newly hatched insects, flew off
on startled wings.

"Mom! Mom! Come out and see what I found," Josh yelled
at the top of his lungs, when he got closer. "I found the perfect
gift for Gramps!"

When Debbie ran out and saw his find, she could hardly
believe her eyes. "Why, Josh, you found Henry! Look, you can
still read the name 'Danny, 4/18/45' written on his back. There
is no doubt that this is Henry, but I can't believe it's possible."
She shook her head in amazement.

"Believe it, Mom. I have the proof right here in my hands,"
Josh told her. "And boy, will Gramps ever be surprised!"

Well, the birthday reunion was a great success. After a lot
of eating and visiting, it was finally time for gifts. There were
new shirts, new socks, a new robe, and countless other gifts.
Then Lizbeth recited her poem, and everyone gave her a standing ovation. Finally, Josh came forward carrying a shoe box.
I could hardly wait to see what was in it.

"Happy Birthday, Gramps," I heard him say loudly, handing
over the box. "I didn't think this needed wrapping."

We all watched Dan lift the cover off the box and stare
at the contents with an amazed expression. "It can't be," he
finally muttered.

"But it is, Gramps," Josh said insistently. "It really is. See?"

Dan reached into the box and lifted out his gift gingerly.

"Look, everyone, Josh found my old box turtle, Henry.
There is my name and the date I had found him, still on his
back. Where did you ever find him, my boy?"

"In the field, Gramps, close to the creek."

"Pretty near where I had found him, back in 1945. Henry was a youngster back then, like myself. I carved my name on his shell." And as Dan was remembering, we noticed that his face had turned younger, and he looked almost boyish.

"I kept Henry for a couple of years, but then I released him back in the field. I even saw him a couple of times after that, but then I got older and all but forgot about Henry."

"You didn't forget, Gramps. You told me all about him, remember?" Josh said.

"Thank you, my boy, for this wonderful gift of a happy memory. It's the best gift I ever received," Dan finally said, wiping tears from his eyes. "I'm a blessed man, to have such a wonderful family." Then it was time to sing "Happy Birthday," while Henry enjoyed the piece of lettuce that Lizbeth put in the box for him.

Two days later, when it was time to go back to the city, Dan and Josh walked down to the creek together, to release Henry, once again. "I told Henry that we're both getting old now, but I think we may have a few good years left in us," Dan said when they came back to the house to get ready to leave.

"And who knows, we may meet again in the near future." Then he smiled and looked at his tow-headed grandson.

"They say turtles can live to be a hundred, you know," he said, ruffling Josh's hair.

"I know, Gramps," Josh replied, taking his grandfather's hand. "And if the good Lord be willing, so can grandfathers."

And as they got into their vehicles, to drive back to the city, I couldn't help but think that Anne was smiling down on them, from Heaven.

Old Man Moreland

NANCY B. GIBBS

In every neighborhood there is usually one scrooge.

As a little girl, I lived in a neighborhood that can only be described as a paradise for children. With a lake across the street and a creek running beside my house, I experienced many delightful days playing with turtles, tadpoles, and frogs. My mom and dad loved to fish while my brother and I swam and played in the water.

A couple of years after we moved into our new home, the scrooge moved in down the street. His house was located directly on the lake, and when he bought the land for his house, he also bought the property on the lake across the street from my house.

We tried to be neighborly until the day he came for a visit. He talked to my parents and after he left I heard my parents discussing his visit. I didn't know exactly what he had said, but I knew my parents were fighting mad.

They began referring to him as "Old Man Moreland."* At six years old, I thought that was his real name. I didn't know he had another first name. I thought the name fit him so well, because I never saw a smile on his bitter, cold face.

---

*Name changed.

"Old Man Moreland this" and "Old Man Moreland that" was the major topic of conversation around my house for a few months. A neighborhood feud was in full force. I found out that Old Man Moreland didn't want my mother and daddy fishing on his property, nor did he want my brother and me to play in the lake. Since we didn't own any land on the lake, he informed my parents that we were trespassing.

Immediately my father began trying to buy a piece of property on the lake so that we could have legal rights to play there. Fortunately, there was a small plot beside the dam that was for sale. Daddy purchased it, which gave us the opportunity to use the lake like everyone else who owned lots, including Old Man Moreland. That made him very angry and also added fuel to the flame, as far as the way he felt about my family.

We continued using the lake just as we had before, despite Old Man Moreland's protests. Each time we saw him, his face was wrinkled in a frown and his attitude toward life seemed to be so bitter. As a happy little girl, I couldn't understand why he was so angry.

One Easter morning when I awoke, a basket was lying beside my bed. "Quack, quack," said the little white duckling in the basket.

"Ruby!" I screamed. "Ruby is your name." I was so excited.

At first Ruby used to swim in my bathtub. The time came, however, when she needed to go across the street and make the lake her home. She grew up to be such a wonderful duck. I could go to the lake and call "Ruby," and no matter where she was, she came to me, expecting breadcrumbs and crackers. Of course, Old Man Moreland didn't like Ruby.

"I'm gonna shoot that duck!" he said one day, loud enough for me to hear. I ran home, crying uncontrollably. It seemed that Ruby disturbed the fish as Old Man Moreland tried to catch them from his dock.

Ruby loved people and visited with everyone on the lake. She even liked Old Man Moreland, even though he didn't like her. Several times a day, neighborhood moms would bring their children to feed her. I guess you could say that she turned into a neighborhood pet. Fat and fine were the words which described Ruby best.

Early one morning, I was getting dressed to go to school. I heard Ruby happily quacking out at the lake. Of course, there was nothing unusual about that, as it happened every day. The unusual thing was how early in the morning it was. The thought struck me that most kids would be getting ready to go to school and the duck feeding usually began much later in the day.

I ran to my bedroom window, and—lo and behold!—Old Man Moreland was standing on his dock. With a smile on his face and a bread bag in his hand, he was feeding Ruby. She was delighted, and as she was gobbling down his bread she quacked a "Thank you!" after each bite.

I can't say that Old Man Moreland was ever overly nice, but I did see a different person that morning as I peeked out my window. At least I realized that he had the ability to smile.

As I went to school that morning, I waved at him for the first time since the unpleasant visit, and he waved back. "He's not so bad, after all," I thought, as I ran off to school.

I never knew what had happened in his past to make him such a scrooge, but I do know that a duck named Ruby made a difference in the old man's life that morning.

By the way, Old Man Moreland never shot Ruby. She lived many, many years in the lake, bringing happiness to everyone who knew and loved her.

The Sweetest of Bears

T. J. BANKS

She is our Original Settler, the Prototype, the Old Lady, and the surviving Charter Member of Ladies of the Club. She is Kilah Kitten, Ki, and the Star of Stage and Screen. But, most of all, she is Kilah Dee, the Sweetest of Bears.

Tim gave her that name. She was, from the beginning, his cat, just as her sister, Cricket, was mine. "How's my Sweetest of Bears?" he would croon to the tortoiseshell kitten with her orange Phantom mask. Of course, he also called her "a pork-belly legislator" back then because she was a good two pounds heavier than Cricket.

We caught them in my Uncle Allan's dairy barn. Kilah was easy: the boldest of the three barn kittens, she made a bee-line for the meat scraps we'd put out. I caught her just as her muzzle and the meat were getting up close and personal. "A good cat-catcher," my uncle said approvingly. Then he shook his head. "You had to get the best one." We tried for Kitten No. 2, but her siblings were already wise to us and had made for the hay bales. Tim and I figured that our best bet was to head home with our captive and come back a little later when they were off their guard.

Kilah figured *her* best bet was to hide from These Horrible Humans and dove first underneath the tiny Penguin refrigerator, then behind the stand-up radiator in the upstairs bathroom. Tim's parents, who'd come over to greet the new arrival, were treated to a glimpse of a many-colored tigery tail wrapped around the radiator coil nearest the blue-tiled wall. As soon as they left, Tim and I headed back up to the farm. We knew we had to come back with another kitten if we were even to have a prayer of getting this one to tame down any time in the near future.

Tim had his heart set on the all-black fuzzball. "Tam," he called to me from the far side of the barn, "the black kitten's *adorable.*" Problem was, the black kitten also had built-in Nikes on its little pawpads and dove under, over, and around hay bales faster than either Tim or Allan could put one foot in front of the other. Meanwhile, the gray-tiger runt had crept out of hiding and was getting ready to sink her baby fangs into a piece of meat that had fallen into the gutter. I glanced over at Tim and Allan, who were still doing a Keystone Kops chase after the furry little inkblot . . . glanced down at Ms. Runt, who clearly thought she was in Kitten Heaven, what with this great find and no bigger, bossier littermates around to swipe it out from under her. . . . "Oh, well," I thought with a mental shrug and made a lightning grab for the unsuspecting gray-stripey girl. Not for nothing had I spent all those summers up at my grandparents' farm, chasing kittens with my brother Gary and my cousins: before she had time to hiss, the second kitten was in the box and on her way to the suburbs and a new identity as Cricket.

They spent their first 24 hours conferring and hatching escape plans behind the downstairs bathroom toilet. Cricket, hungrier for food and affection, sold out to The Enemy first: she gingerly came out of the bathroom and let us touch her.

She didn't purr—oh, no, she had her principles, what barn did we think *she* had been raised in?—but she'd tolerate a few pats. A *few,* mind you. Kilah, on the other hand, continued to hiss and swear at us for quite some time. Then her feline curiosity got the better of her, and she, too, ventured out to get a better lay of the land.

For the next day or so, the sisters appeared to be taming down just fine: then they discovered the "tunnel" between the waterbed drawers and spent an entire day there. By the time we'd lured them out with tuna fish, they'd reverted to barncatism and wanted nothing to do with us. Every string we dangled for them was pointedly ignored; every hand stretched out toward them was spat at. Tim and I stared glumly at one another. "They hate us," he said. For two long-time cat lovers, it was a bitter moment—I mean, we were in the dust, metaphorically speaking—and we sat there in silence, thinking of the nice fluffy house-bred kittens we'd passed up for The Wild Sisters.

It didn't stay that way, of course: Cricket became my great good friend and Kilah, Tim's. But I honestly can't tell you how or when it changed. Still, by the time I pulled Kilah out of Tim's prized strawberry begonia near the end of August, we were pretty much a unified front. Cricket would eat out of my hand, licking pudding off my fingertips, and let me hold her like a baby when she scorched one of her paw pads on the stove burner or had a bad experience with a tipsy kerosene lamp, followed up by an even worse (from her point of view) experience with bath water. And Tim, the mush, spent, oh, I don't remember how long, walking both girls up and down the cellar stairs—they were skittish about the wide spaces between the old wooden steps—to where he'd moved their litter boxes.

(Eventually, he filled in those spaces, first with bubble-packing, then with pieces of drywall.)

About that strawberry begonia: when I first pulled Ms. Dee out of it, it had only been slightly munched upon; there were still enough green leaves on it to give it that "outwardly respectable" look. But by the same time that next day, it was nothing but sticks. Knowing how proud Tim was of that begonia, I spent the rest of the afternoon trying to come up with a way to break the news to him.

"About that begonia—," I began hesitantly that evening, then stopped short.

Tim jumped into the silence. "That begonia," he declared enthusiastically, "has been with me"—he rattled off a year, which, in *my* rattled state, I didn't take note of. "That begonia has *history.*"

Oh, good, I thought: an opening. "You're right," I deadpanned. "That begonia *is* history."

He was so shocked by the devastation that Hurricane Kilah had wrought—by the *completeness* of it all—he hadn't a sarcastic word left in him. And, in Tim's case, that meant he was very shocked indeed.

Thus began Kilah's career as The Bad Girl. I'm not saying that Cricket didn't have a paw in some of the mischief—it's just that we never managed to catch her at it. Then, too, she had an incredibly innocent round-eyed kitten-face (something that stayed with her all the days of her life). Or, as Tim put it, "Cricket's like"—here, he pulled an exaggeratedly sweet, angelic voice out of his bag of many voices—"'Hi, my name is Cricket,' whereas Kilah's got this black mark on her lower lip that makes it look like she's got a cigarette hanging out of her mouth, and she's there"—he pulled out another voice, a tough street-chick one this time—" 'Yeah, I'm Kilah—what's it to ya?' "

Whatever the real story was, it was always Kilah I caught clawing the loveseat or the good blue chair. And, worse yet, whenever I yelled at her to stop, she'd just kind of slew around and throw this *look* my way, her claws still enmeshed in the upholstery. *"Excuse me,"* the large green eyes remarked. *"You talkin' to me?"* Her brazenness—her sheer kitty *chutzpah*—was such, she'd even sit next to me later on while I cobbled the fabric together as best I could. But it wasn't just *chutzpah:* no, Tim and I always swore that she was checking out my work so that she could rip those stitches out in less time.

There was that matter of that small light over the refrigerator: it was one of those old pull-chain fixtures, and I used to leave it on for Tim the nights he worked late. I started noticing that it was still on in the morning and finally spoke to him about it. "I *did* turn it off," he insisted. But he couldn't explain how the light always happened to be on the next day.

A few days later, however, the answer materialized. I happened into the kitchen and saw Kilah sitting on top of the fridge, angling for the pull-chain. Finally, she caught it and with one good *yank!* turned it on. Satisfied with her work, she leaped down from the refrigerator and went on to other things—terrorizing the surviving houseplants probably. (That was the year she declared war on the jades—which is why all our houseplants now hang from the ceiling whether or not God intended them to hang.)

I told Tim about my discovery that night. "Now," I said half-exasperatedly, half-amusedly, "if she'd only learn to turn it off."

"She could if she wanted to," he retorted proudly.

Kilah was also a hardened catnip abuser. Whereas Cricket could get giddy-pawed barely sniffing it, her sister could toss the herb down with the best of 'em. She was always more of a hellion afterwards, leaping up and clawing innocent hands the instant they touched the stair railings. Of course, she was very big on hands, anyway, and always believed in going for the hand dangling the catnip toy instead of the toy itself. This, Tim claimed, was a sign of her Superior Intelligence: "She knows that if you stop the hand, you stop the toy, too."

But, then, he was like that about his Kilah. Years later, when we were waiting in one of the examination rooms at the veterinary clinic, Tim began to go on and on about how much slimmer she was than her formerly runty sister. Cricket had, in fact, begun to put on weight; but, as I pointed out to him, she had a much smaller frame than Kilah, so the extra pounds had no place to go. The tech, who had just weighed the girls, agreed with me and left. Tim, eager to prove us both wrong, tried to sneak Kilah back on the scale while Dr. Feibel's back was turned: he didn't manage to get her squarely on the scale, though, and both she and it came crashing down. I explained to the vet what my husband had been trying to prove; and the older vet looked at us like we were a pair of nice, friendly lunatics and the cats had more brains between them than we could ever hope to have. "I would've thought she was the bigger one," he said politely, glancing toward Ms. Dee. I shot Tim a smugly triumphant look; and Tim—well, he didn't stick his tongue out at me but looked like he wanted to with all his heart.

The sisters' first couple of years passed relatively uneventfully. We took in a couple of cat boarders—first Sparky, then Buddy—for friends on a temporary basis. The girls were not thrilled by their guests; but instead of going after the intruders together, they'd bitterly (but briefly) turn on each other.

"It's your fault."

"No, it's your *fault*—*they wouldn't be here if you hadn't knocked over that jade plant and then dug it up by the roots.*"

"*Well, it was asking for it. Anyway,* you *were the one who stole the hair-trap from the tub and left it and all that shredded tissue around the human while she was napping.*"

"*Well, it's not like I was going to light a match to the tissue: I was just making a statement. . . .*"

Eventually, they'd settle back down and go about their business, tolerating, if not loving, the boarders. Eleven-year-old Sparky, on the other hand, fell in love for the first, last, and only time in his life when confronted with Kilah's tortoiseshell charms and trailed her devotedly during his stay.

The two-cats-in-the-yard (or, rather, -the-house) equation was a good one and stayed in effect for quite awhile. Then Dervish, Tikvah, and Zorro joined us; and in 1992, after we decided that we'd had enough practice on cats, we had our daughter Marissa. The gang showed no jealousy over the baby: in fact, as Tim told Marissa in her baby book, she "was crying so hard" that first night home from the hospital "that all the female cats—Kilah, Tikvah, and Cricket—started crying with you. It was really funny to see the cats so worried about our new kitten."

There was a cat moratorium of about eight months after Marissa's birth. Then Tim, who'd gone around vehemently insisting, "We are NOT taking in any more cats," adopted Woody, a handsome young black-and-white stray who'd been sweet-talking him out in the garden, and Boris, an older tattered-eared, down-on-his-luck red tabby, adopted us. The sisters had mellowed considerably since the Sparky-and-Buddy days (Kilah had pretty much given up the catnip) and took it all in their tigery stride. Cricket ruled quietly but firmly from her office on top of the cupboards in the cellar with the able- (and double-) pawed Tikvah supplying police force when necessary.

Kilah was involved in affairs of state, too, of course, but not to the extent that the other Ladies of the Club were. "It's a Kilahdeelian quality-of-life issue," Tim would say with mock solemnity; and "Kilahdeelian" really did seem to describe the slightly detached, philosophical attitude that she adopted as she matured and left her bad-girl image behind her. Of course, she could and did still wreak havoc on unsuspecting plants. Once, I saw her wake up from a sound sleep on the third floor (where I was working) and glide all the way down to the first floor; there was a shout from Tim, and when I got down to the kitchen, he was trying to defend one of his sea onions from the Wrath of Kilah. He had taken the plant down while he was removing what he called "the garbage-bag-brown paint" that earlier owners had inflicted upon the kitchen; and Kilah somehow *knew* in her sleep that there was an unprotected plant down there that was hers for the taking. Strange but true.

Between Marissa and "the Gang of Seven," Tim's work and various projects, and my writing, our world was humming along very nicely, thank you. And then that world spun off its axis. On the evening of July 11, 1995, Tim was killed instantly when his company van hydroplaned and hit a telephone pole on his way home. The weeks and months that followed are still too painful to look back on for long: it was then that I learned that grief can imprint itself on your body, lodging there like a parasite so that long after the initial trauma has passed, the least upset can trigger it off again, setting off nausea and other intense physical symptoms. An emotional Star 69, if you will.

Marissa was too young to understand much of what was going on, of course: at three-and-a-half, she could only prattle after the graveside service about all the "chairs. And there was a chest. The chest went down." But the cats surprised me by acting as if nothing had changed. As if Tim hadn't gone any-where. Remembering what a cat person Tim had been—re-membering how he'd loved them all, especially his Kilah Dee and Woody ("Just looking at him makes me smile," he'd say of his black-and-white guy with "the aerial view of Stonehenge" on his back)—remembering how my old tuxedo cat Jason had mourned my dad, searching for him for weeks after his death back in 1983—I just didn't get it. Then I realized that he *hadn't* left us. Not completely, anyway. Some essential part of Tim—call it his spirit, his ghost, his presence—lingered in this house of ours like a benediction, causing my friend Sue to say as she stood in the living room weeks after the tragedy, "You know, this is still a happy house. After everything that has hap-pened, it's still a happy house." And the cats sensed it. His Kilah didn't have to go looking for him: he was there, and she knew it. Just as she'd known about that plant years earlier.

But, cat or human, each loss hits us differently. When Cricket died two years later (two days after the anniversary of the accident, in fact), I watched Kilah withdraw into herself. She didn't do any kitty banshee wails or go searching for Cricket, any more than she had for Tim; but it was clear that this loss was too much for her to bear. Maybe Cricket's spirit had moved on faster than Tim's—after all, she had died after four months of kidney trouble, not suddenly or violently, as he had—or maybe the sisters had just been so close, her death was like losing a paw for Kilah, locking her into that terrible sadness. All I knew was that looking into those huge green eyes, I saw a soul as bereft as mine.

It was a kitten—a big-eyed blue tortoiseshell who bore no

physical resemblance to Cricket except for her plushiness and an endearing little lopsided white splotch on the left side of her chin—who brought Kilah out of the wasteland. Keisha is much less shy than Cricket was, but her personality is uncannily like the old Czarina's, something that the other cats seemed to perceive immediately. Star, the Siamese prima donna, loathed her at sight (and Keisha reciprocated 110%), just as she had the older barn cat, and Tikvah, who'd been something of a soul sister to Cricket, gave the kitten the double-pawed seal of approval that she gave to precious few other felines of her acquaintance. But what happened between Kilah and Keisha was as moving as any James Herriot story.

The kitten went directly to the 11-year-old tortoiseshell— walked through the walls of grief, so to speak—and claimed her as a sort of surrogate mom-cat. And Kilah, who'd never mothered a kitten of her own, took her in. Perhaps Keisha touched off some latent maternal instinct of hers. Or perhaps she, like the other cats-in-residence, simply recognized a cat-soul cut from the same cloth as her beloved sister.

Whatever the reason, they were almost always together after that, the younger cat resting her head affectionately on Kilah's back or butt, whichever happened to be more convenient. And Kilah would let her. I'd come across them, napping together on the kitchen radiator or counter, draped over each other, just like the two sisters used to be. And sometimes Kilah would glance up at me, and her eyes would say it all: *I don't hurt anymore. She's not Cricket—I know that—but she's pretty good, you know?*

Three years later, they're still paw-in-paw with each other. I take my earlier words back: it's a much more moving story than any Herriot, with all his skill and all his feeling for animals, ever wrote. To me, at least. You see, I saw it all unfold right before my own eyes—proof positive that sometimes another soul can reach out to ours, past the grieving, and bring us safely back to shore.

It is, after all, as my Tim would say, a Kilahdeelian quality-of-life issue.

A Gathering of Friends

GARY KOWALSKI

Mix a pack of dogs, two dozen cats, several guinea pigs and a jar of earthworms with a 40-voice choir, and what do you get? At the Vermont church where I am the minister, we call it "Blessing of the Animals." Some folks thought I was nuts the first time I invited congregants to bring their pets to church. We'd just renovated our building and installed $40,000 worth of new carpet. Wasn't this an accident waiting to happen? Happily, experience has shown otherwise. The dogs do sing off-key during the hymns, but so far our guests have been very well behaved and seem to know they are part of a special occasion.

Our service is usually held the first Sunday in October, near the feast day of Saint Francis, about whom a biographer wrote: "He overflowed with a spirit of love . . . for dumb animals, reptiles, birds, and any other creature with and without consciousness." A minister friend of mine who's served several small country parishes in England says that people there asked him to bless their plows every year, so it's reasonable to presume that pigs and chickens also received the vicar's prayers in days of yore. But nowadays not many of us depend on animals for our livelihood, so our service is not so much about asking God to bless Tabby and Fido as about acknowledging the ways that animals enrich and bless us.

The Bible says that animals were created to ease Adam's loneliness, and one thing that hasn't changed is the warmth of companionship our animals provide. Legally, we may own our pets, but the joy that animals bring into our homes makes them more like family members than worldly possessions. Because they seem so uninhibited and free, animals are also great icebreakers, helping us to overcome our reserve in social situations. Watching people gather with their pets on the church lawn prior to our blessing, I notice that most seem more talkative, relaxed and outgoing than usual. Our animals seem to make us more animated and spontaneous.

Of course, pets can be a nuisance. Smokey, my mixed-breed dog, never tires of digging holes in the lawn, and I have never met another animal so headstrong. He obeys perfectly if there is a biscuit in my pocket, so I know he understands my commands. He even seems to be able to add and subtract fractions, because if I break the biscuit into fragments, he realizes precisely how many pieces are left and ceases to cooperate when he has calculated that the last goodie is gone. He can be totally infuriating at times. And I wouldn't trade him for the world.

Probably Smokey only *seems* to raise my blood pressure, for actually pets are good medicine. Studies show, for instance, that the simple act of stroking a dog or cat, or just holding an animal in one's lap, can slow the pulse rate. People who have pets have a lower risk of heart disease and tend to live longer than those who lack such companionship. One experiment showed that even sitting quietly in front of an aquarium can have positive physiological effects, much like meditation.

In her *Notes on Nursing,* Florence Nightingale observed way back in 1860 that a small pet "is often an excellent companion for the sick, for long chronic cases especially." Today more and more doctors would agree. The Delta Society, a non-profit organization that promotes human-animal interactions, estimates that there are about 2,000 animal-assisted therapy programs operating in hospitals, nursing homes, and treatment centers throughout the United States.

The psychological benefits of caring for a pet can also be enormous. Mary Lou Randour, a therapist who was in clinical practice for 17 years before joining the staff of Psychologists for the Ethical Treatment of Animals (PSYETA), observes that pets offer us a nonjudgmental, accepting presence—the kind of "unconditional positive regard" that provides the therapeutic element in many forms of counseling.

Animals teach us about love, Randour notes in her new book, *Animal Grace* (New World Library, 2000). Bud, for instance, had been rescued as a young kitten by Judy Johnson and her daughter Samantha when he was flea-bitten and weak. As he grew, no cat had ever seemed so attached to the household where he lived or more affectionate toward his owners. But one day a friend of Judy's came to the house with news that the friend's long-ailing husband had just died. Bud crawled into the grieving woman's lap and, when she left the house, Bud followed her home—and stayed. While he could not replace a husband who had died, Bud did bring a new reason to smile into a widow's seemingly shattered existence.

While it's hard to explain Bud's actions, it's also hard not to be inwardly touched by them. Without words, Randour says, animals open us to dimensions of life that are mysteriously transforming. And if it's true that "those who abide in love, abide in God," animals do bring our spirits into closer communion with our Maker.

The affinity we have for animals appears to be built-in, so that as youngsters we naturally gravitate toward other living creatures. Regina Hyland, an evangelical minister whose book *God's Covenant with Animals* is soon to be published by Lantern Books, points out that children and animals have much in common: an innocence and a lack of pretense that seem to radiate goodness. That's why kids and pets tend to bond so closely, and why both can awaken what is childlike and nurturing in ourselves.

Many children have "pets" their parents aren't even aware of—a toad that lives in the garden, for example, may become a confidante and friend. Some years back, a group of librarians surveyed ten thousand schoolchildren to learn what kinds of books kids like best. The category that emerged as tops was "Animals," and the leading books included ones like my own son's favorite, Wilson Rawl's *Where the Red Fern Grows,* the story of a young boy's coming of age as he learns that while everything dies—even his beloved redbone coonhound pups— love survives.

From infancy on, people and animals seem made for each other. As Regina Hyland observes, paradise is a place where we are at peace with all creatures, and shalom is a vision of a kingdom where the lion will lie down with the lamb and a little child will lead them. Human beings, both the books of Genesis and Isaiah seem to suggest, need the presence and partnership of animals to be genuinely happy and complete. And as Reverend Hyland adds, that's not an insight that's true because the Bible says so; the Bible says so because it's true.

So we will continue to bless the animals at my church, and many other churches around the country will do the same, every October. But even more, the animals will continue to

bless us, with their playfulness, their *joie de vivre* and uncom-
plaining good nature. Who knows, maybe I will even get up
the courage to bring my own dog to the service this year. I'm
not completely sure I could trust Smokey to sit still through an
entire church service or not to howl on the high notes. But
when the chips are down, you can almost always count on the
canine character to come through . . . steady and dependable.

from CLARITY

It Was a Bad Idea All Along or How I Came to Bathe a Mouse

THIRZA PEEVEY

There are times when you just know that something is a bad idea before you do it. I was hosing down the wash stall in a friend's barn and I was in a bad mood. Not that hosing the floor on a cold February evening isn't enough to put you in a bad mood, but I had had a rough day anyway. Nothing had gone right, and now I was cold and wet and tired to boot. Nothing seems right when you are that cold. You don't think straight when you are that cold.

I suppose that is why, when I saw the furry gray creature scampering across the stall floor, I turned the hose on it. On hindsight, it seems to have been purely a reflex move, probably born of my own misery and bad mood. All I remember thinking is, "MOUSE! Get it!"

Like I said, I didn't think. When I saw the poor thing curled up and shivering on the wet macadam floor, I was ashamed. I wouldn't hesitate to set a trap for a mouse, but I didn't like to see anything suffer. How could I expect any mercy in life if I couldn't even show mercy to that poor, wee, shivering beastie?

Her shivers were getting more serious. She didn't have long before she expired from hypothermia. I didn't even think. I scooped her up and took her to the house.

My roommate heard me coming. She just knew I was killed by the way I was hollering. I brushed past her and plunged into the bathroom. I did the only thing I could think of. I plugged the sink drain, turned on the hot water and plunged the mouse in. When Jill saw what I had dropped into the sink, her eyes got quite wide. I explained what I had done. Before I finished, she dissolved into gales of laughter.

Now I had a quite warm mouse swimming in circles in warm water in the sink. She seemed quite relaxed and content. "What in the world are you going to do with that mouse?" Jill asked. Her tone was incredulous, but her eyes were sympathetic. She knew how softhearted I was.

"I don't know, get it warm and dry, I suppose."

"You know, if I had seen it, I would have set a trap for it."

"I know, I probably would have, too. I just couldn't see it suffer."

She nodded and sighed. Then she passed me her hair dryer. I scooped the little creature out of the water. It seemed quite calm now, and regarded me with curious eyes. I had never noticed how dainty and graceful they were. I gripped its tail nevertheless as I turned the hair dryer on it. It was momentarily frightened, but soon seemed to enjoy the warm air coursing over it. I carefully dried every hair on its body.

When I came out of the bathroom with it, Jill had resurrected an aquarium from some corner where she had stowed it in case of future need. "I kept hamsters in this when I was a kid. I don't know why I kept it; I just couldn't get rid of it when there was nothing wrong with it. She can stay in it overnight,

but she goes out in the morning. I can't guarantee I won't set a
trap for her if I see her."

I nodded. I understood. Mice aren't exactly friends on a
farm. An hour earlier, I had felt the same. Mice tore out insula-
tion and chewed on wiring. It wasn't unheard of for them to
start fires. They chewed into tack trunks and ruined leg wraps
and saddle pads. They chewed into feed bags and made
messes of ruined feed. They chewed into tractor seats for nest-
ing material and made nests in the engine. I couldn't blame Jill.
But just for one moment, we were all God's creatures. For one
moment, that mouse showed me a quality of mercy in myself
that I hadn't known was there. And for one moment, she had
blown the memory of the bad day away on gales of laughter.
I owed her. She could stay the night in a warm house.

I woke up the next morning better able to face the challenges ahead. The mouse? Well, she escaped during the night.
Jill set a trap, but we never caught her or saw her again. They
say that sometimes we entertain angels unawares. Do you
reckon they could squeeze into a body that small?

The Night Buster
Was a Dolphin

LONNIE HULL DuPONT

In 1996, my husband Joe and I flew from our home in San
Francisco to my parents' home in Florida. My stepdad, who
had raised me since my fifth year and whom I called Dad,
needed a very serious surgery. He was eighty years old and was
told that he had a 50/50 chance of pulling through. It was serious enough that Joe and I kept our return ticket open and
packed clothes that would be appropriate for a funeral.

Mom picked us up at the airport the night before the operation. Their dog Buster was in the car and simply beside himself with joy at seeing us. "This is good," said Mom, nodding at
the dog. "He's been depressed ever since your dad went in the
hospital. These days he stays under a table when we're home."

That didn't sound like Buster at all. A mix of schnauzer,
poodle, and cocker spaniel, he was a friendly, energetic dog
and smart as a whip. A comical-looking thing, his back legs
seemed considerably longer than his front legs, and his short,
stocky body was covered with long black hair and two shocks
of white that streaked diagonally across his face and belly.
This gave him an off-kilter look, and he wore it well. Bright
little black eyes flashed at us from under a lot of eyebrow hair

that sort of stuck out from his face. All this housed an even-tempered and outgoing disposition. And he adored Dad.

My folks had heard about this runt of the litter when he was just old enough to leave his momma. On a whim they went to see him. As soon as Buster the Pup saw Dad, he ran to him. Dad scooped him up, and the little guy curled right up to Dad's breast. Both Dad and the dog were smitten right away.

Not that Buster only loved Dad. He wanted to be cuddled like a baby by Mom each morning, even though he was actually a little too big to be a lap dog. And he truly liked everyone, as long as they weren't encroaching on his territory. To be honest, I loved going home to visit Buster as much as I loved visiting my folks! But Dad was Alpha Dog from the beginning for Buster. And Buster went everywhere with Dad.

Buster was only two years old when I brought my new husband home to my family. Buster growled a little at first at this tall male stranger, but I told Joe to sit down, dangle his arm, and let Buster come to him. After enough sniffing to satisfy himself, Buster brought a toy to Joe with a clear invitation to toss it. Joe took the bait and eventually was rolling on the floor with Buster. From then on, Buster looked to Joe for a good time.

Our second trip home as a couple was a different time Dad was in the hospital. We spent days with him in his room while Buster waited in the car. Buster would rather sit in a car all day than stay home. My husband, who is not one to sit at all, took on the job of taking Buster out of the car for frequent walks.

One afternoon during that time, Joe was gone an entire hour, so I strolled off to look for him. I found him in the station wagon napping with Buster, the two of them lying spoon fashion, both lightly snoring. This was truly a bonding experience for Buster. After that, even though we only visited my folks once or twice a year, Buster was thrilled to see Joe. They would play and play, indoors and outdoors. I would venture to say that at those times Joe was Honorary Alpha Dog #2!

Now we were with Mom at a very difficult time, and on the first night, Buster played with Joe almost frantically. But soon the little guy retreated under a table and stayed there most of the time. He did indeed seem depressed.

On the morning of the operation, we left Buster home. It was a long day of waiting at the hospital until finally the surgeon came to us. He reported that Dad had made it through surgery but was not yet out of the woods. He needed to make it through the night first.

Mom and I were allowed to see Dad for a few minutes. I had seen people unconscious and hooked up to machines after surgery before; nobody looks good at such a time. But Dad looked horrible. Mom and I didn't even speak, we were so distressed. When our time was up, we left, gathered up Joe, and drove home in silence.

It was now dark. In the house, we all quietly readied ourselves for bed. Buster raised himself up to greet us, but that was about all. Soon he scooted back under a table and curled away from us.

Restless, Joe offered to run to the store for a few things, and I stayed behind with Mom. I was concerned about her. It was just before Valentine's Day, and Dad had given her flowers and candy that past week in case he didn't make it through the operation. There sat the roses on the table. I was still kind of a newlywed and felt terribly sad for my Mom who might be losing the love of her life.

We retreated to our bedrooms before Joe returned. I was

exhausted, but I could not sleep. All I could think about was how much I did not want to lose my sweet stepdad, and in particular, how much I didn't want my mother to lose her husband. After tossing and turning for awhile, I gave up. I quietly left my room and then saw my mother was also up, sitting in her chair in the living room. Buster was asleep, stretched out under his table.

"I can't sleep," Mom said.

I curled up on the couch. "Neither can I."

She was crying a little. "He looked so awful."

I nodded. "Yes, he did."

We fell quiet. Soon the front door opened, and Joe came in bearing grocery bags. Buster suddenly came to life and jumped all over Joe. Always willing to play, Joe dropped the bags on the table and joined Buster on the floor.

It's hard to explain what happened in the next few minutes. First I must report that a few weeks before, Joe and I had watched a TV documentary in which dolphins were mimicking humans in water. The dolphins only did what they could physically do, but their trainers would make noises or swim a certain way, and the dolphins would mimic them, clearly enjoying themselves. It was fascinating and fun to watch.

Of course Buster is not a dolphin, and I don't recall ever seeing a dog actually mimic a human. But tonight, as Buster looked to Joe for action, Joe rolled on his back and kicked his legs, and Buster flopped down and did the same. My mother and I squealed with delight.

Now Joe rolled over and lifted his chest up with his legs extended like a seal. Buster did the same. The two of them inched across the carpet this way, bobbing their heads up. Mom and I howled.

Joe flopped back on his back and kicked his legs. So did Buster.

This went on for several minutes, back and forth. Mom and I laughed so hard our sides hurt and tears ran down our faces. When finally Joe got tired, Buster allowed himself to be petted, then he retreated under the table again.

We three humans continued to giggle and giggle until we finally took ourselves down the hall to our beds. Before I went into Joe's and my room, I hugged my mother and said, "That was a gift, wasn't it?"

She agreed. And we all slept a good night.

So did Dad. Our prayers were answered—he pulled through that night and the next. He was going to make it. But during those days, Buster now refused to eat.

On the third day, I stayed home while Mom and Joe went to the hospital. I was reading at the kitchen table when I heard Buster's dog tags. I looked down, and there he sat, looking at me.

"What's up?" I said. "Do you want to go outside?"

No response. He simply looked at me. Well, I thought, I may as well see if he'll eat. I got a piece of leftover steak from the fridge, and he wolfed it down. Heartened, I filled his dish with dog food. He devoured it. I refilled it, and he ate again.

The phone rang as Buster was finishing up. It was Mom.

"Guess what!" she said. "Your Dad just ate for the first time!"

I looked at the dog. "So did Buster."

For the next few days, Buster continued to eat and was a little more himself, though he stayed low-key until Dad came home from the hospital. From then on, Buster took it upon himself never to leave Dad's side. And when Dad passed away four years later, I truly believe that Buster grieved as much as any of us, and he continues to.

But I will always remember the night he set aside his sadness and put on a show for us—a mimicking that he never did before or again—and helped his beloved human family laugh and relax and rest up for a new and better day.

Celebrate the Day

NANCY B. GIBBS

After relocating from a large city to a small town in south Georgia, I discovered how much more friendly people are in a slower moving place. Shortly after we moved, my husband and I were traveling down a country road when a man approaching us in his truck threw up his hand. My husband waved back.

"Who was that?" I asked.

"I don't know," he answered.

"Well, why did you wave at each other?" I inquired.

My husband simply smiled at me. "You'll understand one day," he said.

Back in my old hometown, nobody had time for each other, much less waved while driving down the roadways. Living in an overcrowded metropolitan area was quite different. Fast paced and always in a hurry, the residents very seldom acknowledged the presence of a stranger.

After a few years of living in the small town, the southern hospitality grew on me. I began waving at people because I liked having them return the gesture.

Even though I loved my small-town life, I kept my part-time job back home. Most of my family still lived there, and keeping the position gave me an excuse to visit more frequently.

Early one Monday morning, I exited the interstate and

drove down a busy highway leading to work. I watched the faces of people, as they sped by. Everyone looked so depressed and blue. I wanted to let down my car window and shout, "Celebrate the day, people!" I felt sorry for them. I waved at many of them, but none waved back.

As I drove further along, I approached a packed six-lane highway, located in front of a mall. Not a single car was moving. One of the lights was green, but traffic was at a standstill. I was surprised at not hearing the first horn honking. I wondered what was going on ahead of me. I glanced over at the driver beside me. She was smiling. All around, people were laughing and pointing toward the intersection. Several drivers had exited their cars and were smiling, as well. There were dozens of happy faces, all looking toward one area at the center of the intersection, but no one seemed concerned about the traffic lights. I couldn't see over the pick-up truck, which was stopped in front of me.

I wanted to see what was going on, so I put my car in park, opened the door, got out and looked toward the area. Crossing the busy intersection at a very slow pace, was a mother duck. As she waddled across the street, several baby ducklings followed close behind in a straight line. There, in the middle of one of the busiest sections of the city, during rush-hour traffic, the baby ducklings were changing the way many busy people were starting their week.

After the mother duck and her babies were safely across the street, the traffic resumed. As a car approached me, the driver smiled and waved, even before I had a chance to wave first.

"Who was that?" I instinctively wondered, glancing back. Then I remembered the day, several years earlier, when my husband didn't try to explain the small-town man's kindness.

That day, I understood the reason why he had waved at us. He wasn't too busy to enjoy the simple things of life.

It dawned on me that even in the hustle and bustle of a busy world, a mother duck and several baby ducklings can make many fast-paced people smile. They can take the blues out of a Monday morning and truly make it a day to celebrate.

If the world is truly in need of love, sweet love, a few baby ducklings scattered around the busy cities could definitely help create an environment for that love to bloom.

ACKNOWLEDGMENTS
(continued from page ii)

"I Named Her Molly," by Bertha M. Sutliff, is used by permission of the author.

"Nell, a Cat With a Star Complex," by Carol Wallace, is used by permission of the author.

"The Gift of a Happy Memory," by Renie Szilak Burghardt, is used by permission of the author.

"A Gathering of Friends," by Gary Kowalski, is from *Clarity,* June/July 2000.

AN INVITATION TO
OUR READERS

If you would like to share a true story about an animal in your life, we invite you to send it to us. If you would like more information about the *LISTENING TO THE ANIMALS* series, visit our website at: ltta.tripod.com (no www, please). You can e-mail your story to: ltta@netreach.net, or mail it to LTTA, Box 214, East Greenville, PA 18041.

Some of the stories in this book came from Guideposts readers, just like you, and we welcome your participation in this inspiring series.

A Note From the Editors

This original Guideposts series was created by the Book and Inspirational Media Division of the company that publishes *Guideposts,* a monthly magazine filled with true stories of people's adventures in faith.

Guideposts is available by subscription. All you have to do is write to Guideposts, 39 Seminary Hill Road, Carmel, New York 10512. When you subscribe, each month you can count on receiving exciting new evidence of God's presence, His guidance and His limitless love for all of us.

Guideposts Books are available on the World Wide Web at www.guidepostsbooks.com. Follow our popular book of devotionals, *Daily Guideposts,* and read excerpts from some of our best-selling books. You can also send prayer requests to our Monday morning Prayer Fellowship and read stories from recent issues of our magazines, *Guideposts, Angels on Earth,* and *Guideposts for Teens.*